LEGAL WRITING
EXERCISES

LEGAL
WRITING
EXERCISES

A PRACTICAL GUIDE TO CLEAR
AND PERSUASIVE WRITING
FOR LAWYERS

E. SCOTT FRUEHWALD

Cover design by Monica Alejo/ABA Publishing.

The materials contained herein represent the opinions of the authors and/or the editors, and should not be construed to be the views or opinions of the law firms or companies with whom such persons are in partnership with, associated with, or employed by, nor of the American Bar Association or the ABA Publishing unless adopted pursuant to the bylaws of the Association.

Nothing contained in this book is to be considered as the rendering of legal advice for specific cases, and readers are responsible for obtaining such advice from their own legal counsel. This book is intended for educational and informational purposes only.

Printed in the United States of America.

18 17 16 15 14 5 4 3 2 1

ISBN: 978-1-62722-892-3

e-ISBN: 978-1-62722-893-0

Library of Congress Cataloging-in-Publication Data
Fruehwald, Edwin Scott, 1955–
  Legal writing exercises : a practical guide to clear and persuasive writing for lawyers / E. Scott Fruehwald.
    pages cm
  ISBN 978-1-62722-892-3 (alk. paper)
  1. Legal composition. 2. Law—United States—Language. I. Title.
  KF250.F78 2014
  808.06'634—dc23
                                    2014041423
Discounts are available for books ordered in bulk. Special consideration is given to state bars, CLE programs, and other bar-related organizations. Inquire at Book Publishing, ABA Publishing, American Bar Association, 321 N. Clark Street, Chicago, Illinois 60654-7598.

www.ShopABA.org

I dedicate this book to my brother, Robert Douglas Fruehwald, who has shared the ride with me.

Contents

Preface

Communication is the key to success. No matter how brilliant a lawyer's ideas may be, those ideas will remain unheard if the lawyer cannot communicate them effectively. Consequently, legal writing is a fundamental skill for lawyers and law students.

I have written this book to help lawyers and law students improve their writing. This book is self-contained (the answers to the exercises are located immediately following the exercises). Lawyers in any stage of their career can use it to help improve their writing skills, or they can use it to become aware of what they should correct in the writing of their employees. Law students can employ this tome to improve their writing immediately before law school or while they are taking legal writing. Legal writing professors can adopt it as a supplement in legal writing class. Writing and academic support specialists can use it to help struggling law students. Finally, while I have written this book specifically for lawyers, most of it can be used by anyone who wants to write better.[1]

How is this book different from other books on legal writing? It mainly teaches you editing and writing through exercises. Many books on legal writing have few editing exercises. However, educational researchers believe that the most effective way to learn is through active learning—through doing.[2]

---

1. Legal writing is specialized writing; it has terminology, techniques, and forms of its own. However, the keys to clear and effective writing are the same for legal writing and other types of expository writing. Legal writing is not a foreign language. It begins with the same fundamentals as other types of writing, and it adopts those fundamentals to the needs of legal problem solving.

2. Michael Hunter Schwartz et al., *Teaching Law by Design: Engaging Students from the Syllabus to the Final Exam*, 5, 13 (2009). Although this book is based on recent research in educational methods and cognitive psychology, I will only be discussing theory in the footnotes and then only briefly. For more on how education research and cognitive psychology affects legal education, see generally E. Scott Fruehwald, "How to Help Students from Disadvantaged Backgrounds Succeed in Law School," 1 Tex. A.M. L. Rev. 83 (2013).

Active learning also helps turn items in short-term memory into long-term memory.[3] In addition, educational experts think that repetition helps one retain knowledge in long-term memory; a pattern needs to be retrieved again and again to become a permanent memory or skill.[4] Similarly, the key to becoming a good writer and editor is awareness. Fixing writing problems once you find them is usually easy. The hard part is finding the mistakes in your writing. The exercises in this book will help you develop the ability to find problems in your writing and the writing of others. I believe that the numerous exercises in this book will help you improve your writing much more than books that contain no exercises or only a few exercises.

This book is also different because it covers subjects that other legal writing books don't cover, such as creating emphasis, continuity and flow within paragraphs, continuity and flow between paragraphs, small-scale organization, and taking a holistic approach to writing. Producing clear and effective writing involves much more than being able to change passive voice to active voice and eliminating wordiness. It concerns being able to combine the mechanics of writing with a conceptual (holistic) view of writing.

It is very important that you do the exercises slowly and carefully. One cannot learn superficially. You should make sure that you understand each concept, and, when you make a mistake, why you have made that mistake. In addition, you should make sure that you understand all the answers.

This book begins with an introduction that presents the general principles of clear and effective writing. The remaining chapters deal with the details of editing, progressing from editing sentences to large-scale organization. Chapter 2 concerns active and passive sentences and writing with verbs. Chapter 3 involves editing for wordiness. Chapter 4 teaches emphasis, clarity, and specificity, while Chapter 5 shows how to combine sentences and edit paragraphs. Chapter 6 covers organizing paragraphs and creating coherence. Chapter 7 shows you how to write a small-scale paradigm, and Chapter 8 discusses large- and medium-scale organization. The book

---

3. Duane Shell et al., *The Unified Learning Model: How Motivational, Cognitive, and Neurobiological Sciences Inform Best Teaching Practices*, 11, 23 (2010) ("It appears that when working memory processing attends to something it has temporarily stored, it is more likely to be permanently stored."); *see also* Fruehwald, "How to Help Students," at 86.
4. Shell, *The Unified Learning Model*, at 12.

concludes with review exercises and a glossary. Although I have written this book to be read consecutively, you can skip to a chapter that teaches an editing skill that you are having particular problems with.

I start each of my legal writing classes by telling my students that my goal for the class is to make myself unnecessary. I want them to take what I have taught them and use that to become their own critic of their writing—to become their own legal writing teacher. I hope I can do the same for you with this book.

Chapter 1

Introduction: General Principles of Writing and Editing

Chapter Goals

1. To introduce you to the general principles of writing.
2. To help you understand the three stages of writing.
3. To help you understand the pre-writing stage.
4. To help you focus on the purpose of your writing.
5. To help you focus on your audience.
6. To help you consider the restraints on an assignment.
7. To help you see the importance of planning.
8. To help you think about strategy in persuasive writing.
9. To help you understand the importance of the editing stage.
10. To introduce you to general principles of editing.
11. To help you develop the habit of reading your writing out loud.
12. To help you develop the habit of reading your writing from another's viewpoint.
13. To help you develop a holistic approach to writing.
14. To help you develop the habit of reading your writing carefully.
15. To help you become your own critic.
16. To help you develop the habit of challenging your writing.
17. To help you reflect on your writing.

The best way to become a self-directed learner is to develop attitudes and habits.[1] The first attitude I want you to develop is "I will become a reader-oriented writer." Most authors write for themselves, and they do not give much thought to their readers. As a result, the reader often misunderstands what the author has said. In contrast, successful writers focus on their readers. They know that it is the writer's responsibility to fully communicate his ideas to his reader. A reader shouldn't have to read a passage twice. The second attitude I want you to possess is "I will try to communicate to my reader as fully as possible."

The exercises in this book are intended to help you develop habits so that you will become a reader-oriented writer who fully communicates her ideas to the reader. However, before starting the exercises you need to learn some general principles about writing.

The Three Stages of Writing

Writing consists of three stages: (1) the pre-writing stage, (2) the writing stage, and (3) the editing stage (the post-writing stage). You should spend an equal amount of time on each of these three stages. I will only discuss the pre-writing stage and the editing stage in this section.

The Pre-writing Stage

In the pre-writing stage, you should define the writing's parameters. What is your purpose in writing? Who is your audience? Are there any restraints on the composition? What is your plan?

A paper's general purpose is often obvious. For example, your boss may ask you to write a memorandum on the law of constructive eviction in Virginia. However, can you go into more detail? Has your boss asked you to write the memorandum so that he can learn the general law on constructive eviction, or does the assignment concern a particular case? Should you look just at Virginia law or also at the law of other jurisdictions? If a case

---

1. You are a self-directed learner. If you weren't, you wouldn't have bought this book. Self-directed learners are constantly looking for ways to improve themselves.

is involved, what is the procedural posture? Having a clear picture of the writing's purpose not only saves time, but helps you focus and organize your writing.

Defining your audience is vital. Communication involves two persons: the writer and the reader. Your writing will be significantly different depending on whether it is for a client, a supervising attorney, or a judge. Most clients do not know legal language.[2] In writing for a client, you must explain all unusual terms and even avoid certain terminology. Writing for lawyers and judges also differs. In writing an objective memorandum for your boss, you should present all sides of an issue, so that your boss can assess the strengths and weaknesses of your client's case. When writing for a judge, you want to persuade the judge to rule in your client's favor. While you should not misrepresent the case to the judge, you will want to present the law and facts in the best possible light in order to obtain a favorable judgment for your client.

Third, you need to know the restraints on the writing. A legal writing professor may require a particular format and set a page limit. Court rules may create similar requirements. Moreover, in the real world, there are usually time constraints and sometimes price constraints.

Finally, it is important to plan what you are going to write.[3] You should think about the substance of the writing before you start writing. What do you already know about the subject matter of the assignment? This will help you plan for how much reading you need to do before you start writing. Of course, a lawyer will research the law in the planning stage. After doing the reading and research the lawyer will need to synthesize that research. How do the pieces of the law fit together? Finally, the writer will apply the law to the facts in her head. (Of course, you can also use outlines or charts to help you organize your thoughts.) You should never start writing before you have fully thought through the assignment or problem. Otherwise, your analysis will be poor, your writing will be poorly organized (see Chapters 7 and 8), and your prose will be hard to understand.

---

2. Of course, there are also many different types of clients.
3. For more on the importance of planning as a part of thinking and learning, see Michael Hunter Schwartz, *Expert Learning for Law Students*, 35–53 (Carolina Academic Press, 2008).

Creating a strategy is also an important part of the planning stage for lawyers writing persuasive documents. Which issues will you argue? How will you argue each issue? These questions affect how you organize a document.

Exercise 1-1

Take a brief or other expository document you have recently written. In writing that document, how much time did you spend on the pre-writing stage? Did you consider the purpose? What was the purpose of the document? Did you consider the audience? Who was the audience? What were the restraints on the writing? Were there time constraints? Money constraints? Page limits? Stylistic requirements? How did the restraints affect how you approached the writing?

How much planning did you do before you started writing? Did you complete the research before you started writing? (Of course, you can go back and do additional research while you are writing if there are gaps. However, you should thoroughly research your issue before writing.) Did you synthesize the law? Did you clearly understand the law before you started writing? Did you do the analysis in your head before you started writing? Did the document require a strategy? If so, did you create a strategy before you started writing? How did the strategy affect the organization of the document?

Exercise 1-2

Consider the following problem. Your client wants to sue a department store for false imprisonment. Your client was shopping at a department store. As she stepped into the parking lot, a security guard stopped her, claiming she had stolen some perfume. The security guard took her to the security office, which was a windowless room, and he told her to wait while he got the manager. She heard the guard lock the office's only door as he left. After approximately 15 minutes, the guard returned with the manager. The manager asked to see your client's purse. He inspected the purse, and he concluded that your client had stolen nothing. He apologized to your client, and she went home. When she got home, she cried for an hour. Does your client have a case for false imprisonment?

How would different purposes, audiences, and restraints affect how you would write up the above problem? Assume that, after having met with your client and researched the facts, your boss asked you to write an objective memorandum on the subject. How would this affect the purpose, audience, restraints, and other aspects of planning? Assume that, after having read your memorandum, your boss asks you to write a letter to your client. How would this affect the purpose, audience, restraints, and other aspects of planning? Assume your boss has asked you to write a brief in support of a motion for summary judgment. How would this affect the purpose, audience, restraints, and other aspects of planning?

The Editing Stage

Concerning his approach to musical composition, Maurice Ravel wrote, "But one must spend much time in eliminating all that could be regarded as superfluous in order to realize as completely as possible the definitive clarity so much desired."[4] A critic similarly wrote of Eric Satie's music, "His works might be said to have been completed beforehand, while he meticulously unpicks them, note by note."[5]

These composers' approaches to composition apply to legal writing. When you have finished a memo or a brief, you must carefully edit it (unpick it word by word) to realize the definitive clarity that helps you communicate to your readers. Nobody writes a perfect brief, but you can make that brief communicate better to your readers through the editing process.

Many of the exercises in this book concern the details of editing. However, editing also involves certain general principles. First, you should edit a draft several times, concentrating on different aspects of the writing. For example, the first time through you might focus on whether the ideas are laid out in a logical order and whether the ideas flow together. The second

---

4. Maurice Ravel, "Contemporary Music," in Margaret Long, *At the Piano with Ravel*, 72–73 (Dent, 1973).
5. Jean Cocteau, *Cocteau's World*, 310 (trans. by Margaret Crossland, Dodd Mead, & Co. 1972).

time through, you might concentrate on wordiness, overuse of the passive voice, and awkward constructions.

A key to editing is to <u>read the paper aloud</u>, <u>listening closely to what you are reading</u>. When you read a paper aloud, you will <u>uncover wordiness</u>, awkwardness, choppiness, and lack of coherence and flow. Also, try to stand in your readers' shoes, realizing that your readers will be reading your writing for the first time. You should also reflect on what you've written.

Proper citations are an important part of legal writing because proper citations show your reader that you are a careful writer. This book will not treat citation format in detail. The best sources for citation style are *Harvard Law Review*, *The Bluebook: A Uniform System of Citation* (19th ed., 2010) and the Association of Legal Writing Directors' *ALWD Guide to Legal Citation* (5th ed., 2014).

Finally, proofreading is a vital <u>part of writing</u>. Misspellings, typos, and bluebooking errors subtract from the effect of your writing. When a judge finds numerous proofreading errors in a brief, she will assume that the legal

Consisten use of Caps

research and reasoning is also sloppy. You should proofread any paper you intend for others to read at <u>least three times</u>. You should never depend on spell check because it is incomplete and imperfect.

Exercise 1-3

How much do you edit your writing? Do you have an editing strategy? Did you go through it several times? What do you start with (large-scale organization, proofreading, citation, etc.)? Do you emphasize different aspects of editing each time? Do you see how reading your paper out loud helps you edit? Do you see how putting yourself in your readers' shoes helps your editing? When you've finished your first draft, do you check to see if it corresponds to the parameters you set in the pre-writing stage?

A Holistic Approach to Writing

While learning the mechanics of writing and editing is important, one also needs to view writing as a whole. Writing is not mechanical; it is an art. Knowing all the rules and mechanics of editing and writing will not help you become an excellent writer if you cannot see the big picture and if you can't reflect on what you have written.

The first habit in becoming a holistic writer is to plan very carefully before you start writing, as suggested in the Pre-writing section. Know what you are going to write before you start writing. Do you have in your head what you want to write? Are you confused about anything? Never start writing if you are confused about the substance.

The second habit of becoming a holistic writer is to read what you have written very carefully. Pay attention to everything. Think about what you have written. Be a harsh critic of your writing. Be detail oriented. Don't skim when you edit. As I will develop more fully throughout this book, you need to think about every word, phrase, clause, sentence, paragraph, subsection, and section. Did I use the best word here (the word that best expresses my meaning)? Do the sentences flow together? Is this paragraph unified? Is this section well organized? Is the essay well organized?

The third habit of becoming a holistic writer is to challenge your writing. Question everything you write. Don't accept the first answer; consider alternatives.

The fourth habit of becoming a holistic writer is to read what you have written out loud and really listen. Reading your writing out loud helps you become more aware of what you have written and of the mistakes you have made. It also helps you challenge your writing. You should listen to all levels of your writing, from the word to the whole. Does my writing sound overly formal, or does it sound natural? How does this sentence sound? Do the paragraphs seem to flow together? Does everything I have written in this section belong in this section?

The fifth habit of becoming a holistic writer is to put yourself in the shoes of your reader. One of the hardest things to do is to step outside of your writing and discover the flaws in what you have written. You need to force yourself to adopt an objective view of your writing to become a complete writer. How would my opponent view my brief? How would my partner view this paragraph? How would my legal writing professor critique my writing? Would a judge fully understand what I have written? Would he have problems following my argument? Have I made the judge's job easier?

Finally, when you finish writing you should reflect on what you have done. Ask the big questions. Does the paper say what I intended it to? Is it convincing? Is it well written? Will the reader have any problems following my thoughts? Can I still do better? To be an excellent writer you must develop your inner voice. You must become a writing introvert. You must also be a harsh critic of your writing. One way to help you develop your inner critic is to criticize your writing as if you were your boss (a demanding boss) or a legal writing professor.

In conclusion, there is one question to ask above all others in holistic writing: Have I fully communicated my ideas to my reader as clearly as possible?

Exercise 1-4

Reflect on the following to help you develop your holistic approach to writing.

Who am I? What kind of lawyer am I? What things do I like about being a lawyer? What things do I dislike about being a lawyer? How can I improve myself as a lawyer? Do I strive to do better, or do I take the easier route?

Step back. How do others view me as a lawyer (or as a law student)? Do other people think I am a hard worker? Are they right? Do other people think I am ethical? Are they right? Do other people think I am a good writer? Are they right?

What are my strengths as a writer? What are my weaknesses as a writer? Do I spend time trying to improve my writing? Do I reflect on what I did right after I have finished an assignment?

Do I spend sufficient time on an assignment, or do I rush through it? Do I depend on others to correct my writing? Do I make sure I fully understand the assignment before I start writing? Do I make sure I fully understand the law before I start writing? Do I make sure I fully understand how the law applies to the facts before I start writing? Do I draft an outline before I start writing?

Am I a writer-oriented writer or a reader-oriented writer? If I am not a reader-oriented writer, how can I become one? Am I a detailed-oriented writer? If I am not a detail-oriented writer, how can I become one? Do I devote my full attention to the assignment?[6] Do I allow things to distract me while I am working? How can I concentrate better (focus) on an assignment?

How much do I think about an assignment before I start writing? How can I improve the pre-writing stages of my planning routine?

How much time do I spend on editing? Do I have an editing strategy? How can I improve my editing strategy and routine?

Do I challenge my writing? Do I consider alternatives, or do I accept the first answer or solution? Do I read my writing from the viewpoint of others? Can I step outside of my writing? If not, how can I develop this skill?

When I finish the assignment, do I reflect on how I have written it? Do I think about how I might write the next assignment better?

Do I have an inner writing voice? How can I develop my inner writing voice? Am I a harsh critic of my writing? How can I become a harsh critic of my writing?

Think of an attorney you admire. Why do you admire that attorney? Think of an attorney or legal writer you admire for their writing. What makes him or her a good legal writer?

---

6. The key to learning and thinking is working memory. Working memory has two functions: temporary storage and processing of information. Duane F. Shell et al., *The Unified Learning Model: How Motivational, Cognitive, and Neurobiological Sciences Inform Best Teaching Practices*, 2, 19 (2010). Working memory is devoted to a task when slots are available for input and attention or processing is directed to the slot. *Id.* at 22. However, working memory cannot handle all sensory input that is vying for its attention; according to recent research, working memory has only about four slots. *Id.* at 11, 27. One of working memory's roles is "attention"—to process some of the input and ignore other parts. *Id.* at 11. In other words, attention directs sensory input. *Id.* at 21, 24. Humans can focus attention, and this mainly depends on concentration. *Id.* at 20, 29. Therefore, you should focus on the task when you are working and avoid distractions. This is also why it is dangerous to talk on a cell phone when driving.

Retrieval Exercises

Education scholars believe that the act of retrieving information from your brain causes information in your long-term memory to be retained better than rereading or restudying. In other words, you should be testing yourself on material as you learn it. After reading each chapter in this book, see if you can write down the main principles of that chapter. If you can't, reread the chapter and try again. Repeat the process until you can remember the main principles of that chapter.

Conclusion

Now that you understand the general principles of writing, it is time to learn the mechanics of writing to develop the habits you will need to become a successful writer. However, do not get lost in the mechanics—use them in connection with a holistic approach.

Chapter 2

Active and Passive Sentences and Writing with Verbs

Chapter Goals

1. To help you use verbs properly and effectively.
2. To help you understand the difference between the active voice and the passive voice.
3. To help you understand when to use the passive voice.
4. To help you change passive sentences to active ones.
5. To help you realize the importance of putting the action in the verbs.
6. To help you recognize nominalizations and eliminate them from your writing.
7. To help you avoid overuse of the verbs "to be" and "to have."
8. To help you recognize and avoid complex verb constructions.
9. To help you develop the habit of reading your writing out loud.
10. To help you develop the habit of paying attention to every detail in your writing (close and careful reading).
11. To help you become aware of the problems in your writing.

Use the Active Voice

Compare these sentences:

> The poacher was shot by the farmer.
> The farmer shot the poacher.

Which sentence sounds better?[1]

Most people would say that the second sentence sounds better because it is shorter and more direct. The second sentence is in the active voice. The sentence's subject is doing the acting, and its structure is actor (noun)–verb–supporting material. The first sentence is a passive sentence; the action is being performed on the subject. The actor appears after the verb and is introduced by a preposition.

One way to identify the passive voice is to look for the verb "to be" followed by the past tense. In addition, you should watch for the preposition *by*. Here are some additional examples:

> The deceased was stabbed by the defendant. (passive)
> The defendant stabbed the deceased. (active)
>
> The suspect was slammed against the car by the FBI agent. (passive)
> The FBI agent slammed the suspect against the car. (active)
>
> The bomb was dropped on the target by the crew. (passive)
> The crew dropped the bomb on the target. (active)
>
> It was held that the statute was unconstitutional. (passive)
> The Court held the statute was unconstitutional. (active)

I hope you agree that in each pair above, the active voice sounds better. You should hear that the active voice is more powerful. Also, active sentences are

---

1. As I mentioned in the Preface, you should always read your writing out loud. When you read your writing out loud, you notice things you would have otherwise missed.

usually shorter. As I will discuss in the next chapter, writers should avoid unnecessary wordiness.

Effective writing uses both active and passive sentences. The passive voice may sometimes be preferable, such as where the actor is obvious or where the writer wants the actor to be ambiguous. Consider this example:

> Mistakes were made. (In this example, the person who made the mistakes is hidden to de-emphasize the subject.)

> Mistakes were made by Jim. (In this example, the fact that Jim made the mistakes is de-emphasized.)

> John was shot by Jim. (In this example, I wanted to emphasize John, so I used the passive voice.)

However, overuse of the passive voice can make your writing sound overly formal. In addition, use of the active voice emphasizes the actor. You should only use the passive voice when you have a particular reason to do so.[2]

Exercise 2-1

Which of these sentences are passive?

1. Jackie argued the case for the plaintiff.
2. The judge warned John to not use profanity.
3. John was cited for contempt by the judge.
4. The judge ruled in favor of the plaintiff.
5. The decision was written by Judge Johnson.
6. James Davis was appointed to the Supreme Court.
7. Mary Johnson wrote the brief.
8. The job was completed on time.

---

2. My college English instructor told us that we should use the passive voice no more than 10 percent of the time. I think my rule is better because it allows for flexibility.

9. The brief was revised by her boss. ✓
10. The secretary typed the letter.

Answers

Sentences 3, 5, 6, 8, and 9 are passive. Note that in sentences 1, 2, 4, 7, and 10 the actor appears at the beginning of the sentence. Sentence 3 emphasizes the object, John, rather than the actor, the judge. Rewriting the sentence in the active voice is preferable, unless the writer wants to emphasize John. Sentence 5 also emphasizes the object. The active version of the sentence ("Judge Johnson wrote the decision") is shorter and more direct. Sentences 6 and 8 dispense with the actor completely. This is acceptable when the actor is unimportant or when the writer wants to make the actor ambiguous. Sentence 9 again places the actor at the end of the sentence.

Exercise 2-2

Change the sentences that are passive to active.

1. An answer must be filed within 20 days after the filing of the complaint.
2. A plaintiff must file a reply to a counterclaim.
3. Affirmative defenses must be raised in the answer, or they are waived.
4. The crime was committed by John Smith, who had formerly been Susan's client.
5. Although she had never met Judge Smith, she felt she knew him from the many stories John had told about his experiences in Judge Smith's court.
6. The verdict was read by the clerk.
7. Mary's argument was not understood by the judge; nevertheless, she ruled in favor of Mary's client.
8. For these reasons, the defendant's motion should be denied.
9. The defendant should have asserted the counterclaim in the prior ·ion.

 · judgment was enforced in Kentucky pursuant to the Uniform
 ırcement of Judgments Act.

11. The play was presented by the community theater.
12. Christ was played by Mark.
13. Volunteers made the scenery from old boxes.
14. Shucks provided the lighting, and the music was performed by the community orchestra.
15. The play was enjoyed by everyone, especially the performance of Brad Danner, who was John the Baptist.
16. The accident was seen by many people.
17. Five arrests were made by the police.
18. The testimony was inadmissible.
19. The testimony was ruled inadmissible by the court.
20. After the end of exams, a party was held by the law students.
21. I was invited to the party by Tom.
22. The State of the Union Address was read by the president.
23. John Jones appeared in thirty movies; his brother John, in fifteen.
24. After law school, a job was obtained by Susan at the District Attorney's office.
25. For these reasons, summary judgment should be rendered for the defendant.

Answers[3]

1. The defendant must file an answer within 20 days after the plaintiff files the complaint.
2. No change.
3. The defendant must raise affirmative defenses in the answer, or they are waived. (This sentence contains two independent clauses. In such a case, check both clauses for passive constructions.)
4. John Smith, who had formerly been Susan's client, committed the crime.
5. No change.
6. The clerk read the verdict.

---

3. Note: In these exercises and many of the other exercises in this book, there is often more than one correct answer.

7. The judge did not understand Mary's argument; nevertheless, she ruled in favor of Mary's client.

8. For these reasons, this court should deny the defendant's motion. (Or, The court should deny the defendant's motion for these reasons.)

9. No change.

10. The plaintiff enforced the judgment in Kentucky pursuant to the Uniform Enforcement of Judgments Act.

11. The community theater presented the play.

12. Mark played Christ.

13. No change.

14. Shucks provided the lighting, and the community orchestra performed the music. (Again, there are two independent clauses in this sentence.)

15. Everyone enjoyed the play, especially the performance of Brad Danner, who was John the Baptist.

16. Many people saw the accident.

17. The police made five arrests.

18. No change.

19. The court ruled the testimony was inadmissible.

20. After the end of exams, the law students held a party.

21. Tom invited me to the party.

22. The president read the State of the Union Address.

23. No change.

24. After law school, Susan obtained a job at the District Attorney's office. (Did the original sound particularly clumsy to you?)

25. For these reasons, this Court should render summary judgment for the defendant.

Read each version of the above sentences aloud. Which version sounds better? Remember, you can use the passive voice when you have a reason to use the passive voice.

Exercise 2-3

Edit the following passage to eliminate passive constructions.

The feature paper was presented by John Smith. He argued that capital punishment is wrong because it is not applied uniformly by the state. Minorities and the poor are sentenced to death more frequently than whites or the rich. In addition, proper legal counsel often cannot be afforded by the poor. The only way these inequalities can be eliminated is for capital punishment to be abolished by our legislatures.

Answer

John Smith presented the feature paper. He argued that capital punishment is wrong because the state does not apply it uniformly. Courts sentence minorities and the poor to death more frequently than whites or the rich. In addition, the poor often cannot afford proper legal counsel. The only way the state can eliminate these inequalities is for our legislatures to abolish capital punishment.

Read both of the above paragraphs aloud. Note how the second version sounds more natural and how the sentences seem to flow together. The first version sounds choppy. You probably paused longer at the ends of most sentences in the first version than you did in the second version.

Exercise 2-4

Take a paper you have recently written and eliminate as many passive sentences as possible. Read both versions aloud.

You should now know the difference between active and passive voice, and how to change passive voice to active. You should also know when to use the passive voice. If you are still having problems recognizing passive voice in your writing, repeat Exercise 2-4.

Write with Verbs

Another problem that frequently appears in writing is a tendency to use nouns, adjectives, adverbs, and clauses to do the work of verbs. Consider the following examples.

> Bob drove quickly down the road.
> Bob sped down the road.

> The diplomats worked at normalization of relations between the countries.
> The diplomats tried to normalize relations between the countries.

In the second version of the first pair of sentences, a specific verb replaces the adverb and nonspecific verb of the first version. Not only does the second version eliminate one word, it sounds more direct and powerful. In the second pair of sentences, the first version lets the noun perform the action; action is the function of a verb. Transforming verbs into nouns is called nominalization.

Exercise 2-5

Edit the following sentences to make the verb perform the action. (There may be more than one correct answer.)

1. The homeless man looked at the food in the shop window in a hungry manner.
2. The company's business was the importation of fine china.
3. William ate the meal slowly in order to enjoy it fully.
4. The children had fun at the amusement park.
5. The dancers went across the stage in a snake-like manner.
6. Anne lived life to the fullest.
7. His crime was a big surprise to his friends.
8. He spoke to the crowd in a loud voice.
9. Mack gave a lecture to the child.
10. The court found that the company had committed discrimination against women.
11. John and Mary made a decision about which curtains to buy.
12. The workers achieved completion of the job.
13. Mrs. Smithers told me to make changes in the design.
14. Our leaders must take action now, or a disaster will happen.
15. Bill's employer asked him to make a summary of the new cases.
16. The president needs to take action on the economy.
17. The letter came as a shock to Linda.
18. The tailor made alterations in the pants but not in the coat.
19. Mary made a cut in her paper to keep it under 20 pages.
20. Minorities caused the election of the mayor.

Answers

1. The homeless man hungered for the food in the shop window.
2. The company imported fine china.
3. William lingered over the meal in order to enjoy it fully.
4. The children enjoyed the amusement park.
5. The dancers slithered across the stage.
6. Anne savored life.
7. His crime shocked his friends.
8. He screamed at the crowd.
9. Mack lectured the child.
10. The court found that the company had discriminated against women.
11. John and Mary decided which curtains to buy.

12. The workers completed the job.
13. Mrs. Smithers told me to change the design.
14. Our leaders must act now, or a disaster will happen.
15. Bill's employer asked him to summarize the new cases.
16. The president needs to act on the economy.
17. The letter shocked Linda.
18. The tailor altered the pants but not the coat.
19. Mary cut her paper to keep it under 20 pages.
20. Minorities elected the mayor.

Don't the revisions sound better? Can you see why?

Exercise 2-6

Eliminate the nominalizations in the following sentences.

1. Jane will make a decision as to whether she will attend law school.
2. The salesman made a demonstration of the company's new oven.
3. The company made full disclosure of defects in the automobile.
4. The court's denial of Jane's motion was because it was filed too late.
5. The company made a request to Peter that he transfer to the Denver office.
6. The government's enforcement of the statute was strict.
7. The court's determination was that the will was revoked.
8. Mike's assumption was that she didn't like him.
9. The assignment from the teacher was to read chapter five.
10. Debbie's promotion came through yesterday.
11. The vagrant's institutionalization was without a hearing.
12. Lee's understanding of the problem was incomplete.
13. Shelley's action was a violation of the act.
14. The doctor's prescription for Barb was a good night's sleep.
15. Roger's failure of the class caused him to be expelled from law school.
16. The conclusion of the police was that Martha's failure of observation of the stop sign was the causation of the accident.

17. Cindy's attempt to make the team failed.
18. Nancy wanted acceptance from the group.
19. The violinist's performance consisted of Beethoven's Violin Concerto.
20. A failure to maintain a C average will result in your dismissal from law school.

Answers

1. Jane will decide whether she will attend law school.
2. The salesman demonstrated the company's new oven.
3. The company fully disclosed the defects in the automobile.
4. The court denied Jane's motion because it was filed too late.
5. The company requested that Peter transfer to the Denver office.
6. The government strictly enforced the statute.
7. The court determined that the will was revoked.
8. Mike assumed that she didn't like him.
9. The teacher assigned them chapter five to read.
10. Debbie was promoted yesterday. (Or, to avoid the passive, The company promoted Debbie yesterday.)
11. The vagrant was institutionalized without a hearing. (Or, The state institutionalized the vagrant without a hearing.)
12. Lee incompletely understood the problem.
13. Shelley violated the act.
14. The doctor prescribed a good night's sleep for Barb.
15. Roger failed the class, causing him to be expelled from law school. (Or, Roger was expelled from law school because he failed the class. Or, Because he failed the class, Roger was expelled from law school.)
16. The police concluded that Martha caused the accident by running the stop sign. (Sentences can contain multiple nominalizations.)
17. Cindy failed to make the team.
18. Nancy wanted to be accepted by the group.
19. The violinist performed Beethoven's Violin Concerto.
20. If you fail to maintain a C average, you will be dismissed from law school.

Note how the original versions of the sentences sound formal and stiff in comparison to the corrected ones. This is especially true when you read them out loud.

Exercise 2-7

Look for nominalizations in a paper you have recently written or in the newspaper.

Pointers

1. You should check your writing to make sure you are putting the action in verbs rather than in nouns, adjectives, adverbs, or clauses.
2. You should look for nominalizations in your writing and eliminate them.

Exercise 2-8

Use the techniques of this chapter to edit the following passage.

The occurrence of the accident was at Fifth and Main. At approximately one-fifteen, a white Mustang was smashed into by a red Toyota. Although it was determined by the police that the Mustang was speeding, their conclusion was that the cause of the accident was a failure of the Toyota's brakes. Badly worn brakes were found by the investigators in the Toyota. The driver of the Toyota was issued a citation by the police. Otherwise, no charges were filed by the police, probably because no one was injured and property damage was minimal.

Answer

The accident occurred at Fifth and Main. At approximately one-fifteen, a red Toyota smashed into a white Mustang. Although the police determined that the Mustang was speeding, they concluded that brake failure caused the accident. Investigators found badly worn brakes in the Toyota. The police cited the driver of the Toyota. Otherwise, the police did not file charges, probably because no one was injured and property damage was minimal.

Don't Overuse the Verbs "To Be" or "To Have"

The verb "to be" is the most common verb in the English language. However, overuse of "to be" can make your writing sound weak. Consider the following paragraphs:

Martha is a lawyer in a large New York law firm. She is one of the brightest young lawyers in the firm. Her area of practice is employee benefits, and her boss is Mary Smith. Martha is happy with her job.

Martha works in a large New York law firm. She is one of the brightest young lawyers in the firm. She practices in the area of employee benefits, and she works for Mary Smith. Martha enjoys her job.

The first version is choppy and dull because of overuse of the verb "to be." The second version contains more verb variety and sounds better. It is not wrong to use the verb "to be"; it is wrong to overuse it. The same applies to "to have."

Exercise 2-9

Change the "to be" or "to have" verbs in the following sentences to active verbs.

1. John is a lawyer.
2. Laura's home is Lexington, Kentucky.
3. Professor Smith has an old Datsun.
4. Nan has a poodle.

5. The sunset is beautiful.
6. Jan will have her first jury trial in June.
7. There will be a clown at the party.
8. Donna was in Europe last summer.
9. My job is in the criminal division of the Attorney General's office.
10. Her dream is to climb Mt. Kala.
11. The smell of the roses is sweet.
12. Bob was not at work today because of tomorrow's test.
13. This case is about the 1st Amendment.
14. The castle is on the mountain.
15. Linda had a red hat on.
16. Mike has knowledge of the murderer's identity.
17. Her opinion is that the case should be settled.
18. The states do not have copyright laws because of federal preemption.
19. They have a beach house.
20. The price of the vase is 20 dollars.

Answers

1. John practices law.
2. Laura lives in Lexington, Kentucky.
3. Professor Smith drives an old Datsun.
4. Nan owns a poodle.
5. The sunset looks beautiful.
6. Jan's first jury trial will occur in June. (Or, Jan will conduct her first jury trial in June.)
7. A clown will perform at the party.
8. Donna visited Europe last summer.
9. I work in the criminal division of the Attorney General's office.
10. She dreams of climbing Mt. Kala.
11. The roses smell sweet.
12. Bob skipped work today because of tomorrow's test.
13. This case concerns the 1st Amendment.
14. The castle sits on the mountain.
15. Linda wore a red hat.
16. Mike knows the murderer's identity.

17. She believes that the case should be settled.
18. The states lack copyright laws because of federal preemption.
19. They own a beach house.
20. The vase costs 20 dollars.

(I realize that the above exercises seem very simple. However, the point of the exercises is to help you recognize the problems in your writing. The hardest thing in writing is often recognizing what needs to be fixed. Once you find the problem, the fix is often simple.)

Pointer

Examine your writing for overuse of the verbs "to be" or "to have."

Avoid Complex Verb Constructions

Writers should avoid complex verb constructions whenever possible. Such constructions frequently involve the verbs "to be" or "to have."

The dog had to have a bath.
The dog needed a bath.

He needed to have an operation.
He needed an operation.

She thought she would have become a doctor by now.
She thought she would be a doctor by now.

She thought she would have been married by now.
She thought she would be married by now.

I'm sure the first example in each pair above sounds bad to you. I am also sure that similar problems sometimes appear in your writing.

Also, one should reserve words such as *could*, *would*, *can*, *may*, and *might* for circumstances concerning uncertainty. Overuse of these words weakens your writing.

Exercise 2-10

Eliminate the complex verb constructions in the following sentences.

1. Most historians consider him to have been the most important poet of his generation.
2. The child had to have a cookie.
3. Joe Johnson was thought to have been a part of the Lincoln conspiracy.
4. Before his early death, Smith was to have been the next president.
5. A child needs to be loved.
6. The expectant parents wanted to have a girl.
7. James would have been 40 today if he hadn't had been killed in the accident.
8. She wanted to be young again.
9. By this time next year, I will have been retired for six months.
10. You should have come to swim instead of just sitting by the pool.

Answers
1. Most historians consider him the most important poet of his generation.
2. The child craved a cookie. (Always pick the best word that conveys your meaning.)
3. Joe Johnson was probably a part of the Lincoln conspiracy.
4. Before his early death, Smith was chosen as the next president.
5. A child needs love.
6. The expectant parents wanted a girl.
7. James would be 40 today if he hadn't died in the accident.
8. She yearned for her lost youth.

9. I will retire in six months.
10. You should have swum instead of just sitting by the pool.

Pointer

Examine your writing for complex verb constructions.

Exercise 2-11

Write several paragraphs, paying careful attention to the verbs you use. Next, rewrite these sentences using passive voice, weak verbs, "to be," and complex verb constructions. Read the two versions aloud, noting especially how the sentences flow together and where the emphasis in the sentences lies.

Now that you have finished the first chapter of exercises, do you feel that you are looking at your writing more carefully?

Chapter 3

Editing for Wordiness

Chapter Goals

1. To help you recognize unnecessary words and wordy expressions in your writing.
2. To help you eliminate unnecessary words and wordy expressions in your writing.
3. To help you recognize unnecessary repetitions in your writing and eliminate them.
4. To help you recognize unnecessary "there" and "it" constructions in your writing and eliminate them.
5. To help you recognize long descriptive phrases in your writing and eliminate them.
6. To help you recognize wordy negative expressions in your writing and eliminate them.
7. To help you shorten introductory phrases.
8. To help you develop the habit of thinking about every sentence, clause, phrase, and word you write.

Edit Wordy Expressions

A major problem with much writing is wordiness—using several words when one will do. Readers get stuck in long sentences containing excess verbiage. A lawyer can often improve his or her writing considerably just by paring unnecessary words. I usually can cut at least 10 percent from a first draft just by eliminating wordiness.[1] Read the following examples (out loud):

> In some instances, even people who are well educated will make mistakes that are serious.
> Sometimes, even well-educated people will make serious mistakes. (better)

> The question as to whether summary judgment should be granted by this court will be dependent upon factors that are difficult for a judge to decide.
> Whether this court will grant summary judgment will depend upon difficult factors for the judge. (better)

I hope that you liked the second versions better. They are shorter and easier to read because they contain fewer words. (I hope you noticed that I included the passive voice and a nominalization in the second example. They also create wordiness.)

To find wordiness in your writing, you need to slowly and carefully read your writing. You should consider every sentence, clause, phrase, and word you've written to determine whether you can eliminate words without changing the meaning.

Exercise 3-1

Edit the following sentences for wordiness.

1. I am writing you in regard to your letter of March 5, 2014.
2. John is a person who succeeds at everything he does.
3. Mary left in an abrupt manner.
4. Owing to the fact that he was ill, Barry did not go to work.
5. Many people here in the city of Louisville enjoy horse racing.

---

1. Eliminating wordiness comes in handy when you have a page limit.

6. Students use the library for research purposes.
7. She lives in the vicinity of Chicago.
8. He acted in a suspicious manner.
9. In the last few days, she recently decided to attend law school.
10. He studied abroad in France.

Answers

1. I am writing you regarding your letter of March 5, 2014. (Or, I am writing you about your letter of March 5, 2014.)
2. John succeeds at everything he does.
3. Mary left abruptly.
4. Because he was ill, Barry did not go to work.
5. Many people in Louisville enjoy horse racing.
6. Students use the library for research.
7. She lives near Chicago.
8. He acted suspiciously.
9. In the last few days, she decided to attend law school. (Or, She recently decided to attend law school.)
10. He studied in France.

The above answers corrected two types of problems. Some answers substituted one or two words for several. Others eliminated redundant words or phrases. (Notice that the original versions of sentences 3, 6, and 8 used an adjective and manner or purpose. Always examine phrases that contain adjectives and manner, purpose, fashion, style, or similar words for wordiness. In such instances, change the adjective to an adverb and eliminate the noun.)

Did any of my changes in the above exercises change the meaning of the sentences? Don't eliminate words if doing so will change the meaning. Also, sometimes you might want to use a longer expression for variety.

The following chart lists common wordy expressions.

Wordy Expressions and Structures	Possible Substitutes
on account of	because

Wordy Expressions and Structures	Possible Substitutes
in view of the fact that	because
in instances in which	when
in some instances	sometimes
in spite of the fact that	although
in all likelihood	probably
as of	beginning
as yet	yet
alongside of	alongside
in a (suspicious) manner	(suspiciously)
in a (sly) fashion	(slyly)
of a (hostile) character	(hostilely)
is of importance	important
in a (loud) way	loudly
in many cases	often
of a (jealous) nature	(jealously)
due to the fact	because, since
owing to the fact	because, since
based on the fact that	because, since
for the reason that	because
the reason why is that	because
in favor of	for
at this point in time	now
during the time	during
until such time as	until
time period	time
in regard to	about, regarding
in order to	to
in terms of	avoid completely
kind of	avoid completely
sort of	avoid completely
one of the most	avoid completely
in relation to	about
by means of	by
in that case	then

Wordy Expressions and Structures	Possible Substitutes
with the exception of	except
give an indication of	indicate
the question as to whether	whether
have an impact upon	affect
she is a person who	she
in the vicinity of	near
in the neighborhood of	near
pertaining to	about
highly unlikely	unlikely
for (research) purposes	for (research)
the editing of newspapers	newspaper editing
(John), who is (Bill's son),	(John), (Bill's son)
several of (the people)	several (people)
a number (of solutions)	numerous (solutions)
some of the (people)	some (people)
a lot of (people)	many (people)
a large number of (students)	many (students)
a large percentage of (women)	many (women)
a variety of solutions	several (solutions)
those kinds of	those
large in size	large
together with	together
join together	join
recur again	recur
it may be recalled that	avoid completely
it is clear that	avoid completely
it would appear that	avoid completely
The city of (Albany)	(Albany)
(Albany), which is in (New York)	(Albany, New York)
the level of (wages)	(wages)
the level of the (water)	the (water) level
in the area of (contracts)	(contracts)
the purpose of this paper	this paper's purpose
the concept of (property)	property

Wordy Expressions and Structures	Possible Substitutes
the fact is	avoid
will in the future	will
the book of John	John's book
utilize	use, employ
-wise	avoid completely

Notice how many of the wordy phrases above end with the preposition "of." Also note that many of the wordy phrases begin and end with prepositions (compound prepositions). Often, you can substitute one word for a wordy prepositional phrase.

The list is not exhaustive; numerous additional wordy expressions exist. You should closely examine your work and pare all wordy expressions. Of course, you should not change a passage's meaning for the sake of brevity. Also, make sure that every word you write, especially adverbs and adjectives, adds something to the sentence. You should make every word count.

You can also eliminate words by changing clauses into phrases. You should watch especially for clauses that contain *who*, *which*, or *that*. Consider the following examples:

> While the play was going on, Lisa slept.
> During the play, Lisa slept. (better)
> Lisa slept during the play. (even better)

> Margaret, who was Watson's sister, came to the party.
> Margaret, Watson's sister, came to the party. (better)

> The vase that is on the self once belonged to John Adams.
> The vase on the shelf once belonged to John Adams. (better)

> The court reversed the errors, which were made by the lower court.
> The court reversed the errors made by the lower court. (better)
> The court reversed the lower court's errors. (even better).

Exercise 3-2

Edit the following sentences using the above list and other hints from this and earlier chapters.

1. John is a person who likes to have fun.
2. He took an umbrella to work due to the fact that it was raining.
3. Her phone call was in regard to the Davis case.
4. A bedroom is for sleeping purposes.
5. Nancy proposed a number of solutions for Jack's roommate problem.
6. Judy lives in the city of Dayton, which is in the state of Ohio.
7. He left the party in an abrupt manner.
8. Based on the fact that he hates pasta, Larry didn't join us for dinner.
9. He lives in the neighborhood of the law school.
10. Owing to the fact that several of the students failed the property test, Professor James gave a test for makeup purposes.
11. The level of the water in the river is at flood stage.
12. The principal canceled school on account of snow.
13. A large percentage of women support the law.
14. In view of the fact that he had been drafted, Martin wrote a will.
15. The bad economy has had an impact on home sales.
16. The school will in the future add a program in health law.
17. Those kinds of teenagers frequently smoke pot.
18. All my friends came to my party with the exception of Peggy.
19. The level of wages remained steady last year.
20. Our lawyers suggested a variety of solutions.
21. The package, which he had been expecting for several days, arrived on Friday.
22. Pursuant to the terms of the contract, the buyer must pay invoices within seven business days.
23. The judgment, which had been entered by the lower court, was reversed by the Supreme Court.
24. In the event of rain, we will move the party inside.
25. Prior to this case, the state had applied contributory negligence.

26. The right of free speech, which is guaranteed by the 1st Amendment, applies only against the government.
27. The ruling of the judge was that the evidence was inadmissible.
28. The verdict of the jury was guilty.
29. The second clause does not affect the claim of the stockholders.
30. While taking a nap, Sylvia dreamed about the accident.

Answers

1. John likes to have fun.
2. He took an umbrella to work because it was raining.
3. Her phone call was about the Davis case.
4. A bedroom is for sleeping.
5. Nancy proposed several solutions for Jack's roommate problem.
6. Judy lives in Dayton, Ohio.
7. He left the party abruptly.
8. Because he hates pasta, John didn't join us for dinner.
9. He lives near the law school.
10. Because several students failed the property test, Professor James gave a makeup test.
11. The river is at flood stage.
12. The principal canceled school because of snow.
13. Many women support the law.
14. Because he had been drafted, Martin wrote a will. (Or, Martin wrote a will because he had been drafted. Use the version that sounds best in context.)
15. The bad economy has affected home sales.
16. The school will add a program in health law.
17. Those teenagers frequently smoke pot.
18. All my friends came to the party except Peggy.
19. Wages remained steady last year.
20. Our lawyers suggested several solutions.
21. The package he had been expecting for several days arrived on Friday.
22. Under the contract, the buyer must pay invoices within seven business days.

23. The Supreme Court reversed the lower court's judgment. (wordy and passive)
24. If it rains, we will move the party inside.
25. Before this case, the state had applied contributory negligence.
26. The right of free speech, guaranteed by the First Amendment, applies only against the government.
27. The judge's ruling was that the evidence was inadmissible. (Even better: The judge ruled that the evidence was inadmissible.)
28. The jury's verdict was guilty.
29. The second clause does not affect the stockholder's claim.
30. During a nap, Sylvia dreamed about the accident.

Each change above is small. However, you can significantly improve the readability of your writing when you make these changes throughout a paper.

As was true of the writing problems I discussed in the last chapter, eliminating unnecessary words is easy once you can recognize them in your writing. This is why you have to change how you read your writing—be a careful reader. (Did you notice that Larry was accidently changed to John in number 8? You need to be aware of every detail.)

Pointers
1. Read every sentence, clause, phrase, and word to eliminate wordiness in your writing.
2. Do not make changes if the changes affect the meaning or if you have some other reason not to make the changes.

Eliminate Unnecessary Repetitions

Wordiness also occurs because of unnecessary repetitions. Consider the following sentence: He left suddenly in an abrupt manner. A writer should eliminate either "suddenly" or "in an abrupt manner" because they say the same thing. He left abruptly, or he left suddenly.

Exercise 3-3

Eliminate the unnecessary repetitions in the following sentences.

1. The weather here in Louisville is beautiful.
2. Each and every person should attend his lectures.
3. Her painting was beautiful in appearance.
4. His presentation was equally as good as John's.
5. She is shorter in height than her sister.
6. The car was a blue color.
7. I personally have never been to Europe.
8. The weather will probably continue to remain cold.
9. The professor allowed him to retake the test again.
10. The spacecraft was oval in shape.

Answers
1. The weather in Louisville is beautiful.
2. Every person should attend his lectures. ("Each and every" is common in legal writing. It adds nothing to the meaning.)
3. Her painting was beautiful.
4. His presentation was as good as John's.
5. She is shorter than her sister.
6. The car was blue.
7. I have never been to Europe.
8. The weather will probably remain cold.
9. The professor allowed him to retake the test.
10. The spacecraft was oval.

Can you see how the unnecessary repetitions in the original sentences add nothing to the meaning?

Another source of wordiness is unnecessary repetition of a word or phrase in a sentence.

The drive will take two days or three days.
The drive will take two or three days.

The attack will come by land, by sea, or by air.

The attack will come by land, sea, or air.

Exercise 3-4

Eliminate the unnecessary words or phrases in the following sentences.

1. Mark likes 18th-century music and 19th-century music.
2. Susan's hair was black; Mary's hair was blonde.
3. You will succeed by working hard, by living frugally, and by caring about others.
4. John likes his classes during third period and fifth period.
5. Kevin liked Anne because she was smart, because she was kind, and because she was polite.
6. Jim had five dollars, Jack had four dollars, and Jill had six dollars.
7. Sally had a yellow sports car, and Joe had a red sports car.
8. You cannot go to the party until you do your homework and until you clean up your room.
9. The class accepts children who are five-years-old, six-years-old, or seven-years-old.
10. A student can complete the degree in three years, in four years, or in five years.

Answers

1. Mark likes 18th- and 19th-century music.
2. Susan's hair was black; Mary's, blonde.
3. You will succeed by working hard, living frugally, and caring about others.
4. John likes his third- and fourth-period classes.
5. Kevin liked Anne because she was smart, kind, and polite.
6. Jim had five dollars, Jack four, and Mary six.
7. Sally had a yellow sports car, and Jim had a red one.
8. You cannot go to the party until you do your homework and clean up your room.

9. The class accepts children who are five-, six-, or seven-years-old. (Or, The class accepts five-, six-, or seven-year-old children).

10. The student can complete the degree in three, four, or five years.

(Did you catch the mistakes I made in rewriting the fourth and seventh examples? A careful reader would have.)

Pointer

Eliminate unnecessary repetitions.

Eliminate "There" or "It" Constructions

Constructions using *there* or *it* may produce wordiness. For example: "There are many people who like classical music." "Many people" is the subject of this sentence; "there are" is unnecessary. One can rewrite this sentence as follows: "Many people like classical music."

"It is apparent to everyone that Mary committed the crime." The phrase beginning "it is" is unnecessary. The sentence means the same thing if "it is" is deleted: "Mary committed the crime."

Not all phrases that begin with *there* or *it* are unnecessary. *There* is proper when it is the subject of the sentence. Likewise, *it* is proper when it depicts something definite, as in the following:

There are five reasons to take evidence.
Grapefruit is very healthy. It contains vitamin C.

Exercise 3-5

Eliminate wordy *there* or *it* clauses from the following sentences.

1. It is obvious that John will win the competition.
2. There are many ways to train a dog.
3. There are six subjects the professor might test us on.
4. There are five students nominated for the scholarship.
5. It is probable that it will snow tonight.
6. It is cold in this room.
7. There are at least five women who can win the competition.
8. John told me it is a good book.
9. It is probable that the Giants will win the Super Bowl.
10. There are too many people packed into the concert hall.

Answers

1. John will obviously win the competition.
2. Correct; *there* is the subject.
3. The professor might test us on six subjects.
4. Five students are nominated for the scholarship.
5. It will probably snow tonight.
6. This room is cold.
7. At least five women can win the competition.
8. Correct; *it* stands for a particular book.
9. The Giants will probably win the Super Bowl.
10. Too many people are packed into the concert hall.

Pointer

Eliminate unnecessary *there* and *it* clauses.

Eliminate Long Descriptive Phrases

Another source of wordiness is long descriptive phrases. One can often rewrite long descriptive phrases in one or two words.

> She is a student who works hard.
> She is a hardworking student.

> He was depressed by the weather, which was dark and dreary.
> He was depressed by the dark and dreary weather.
> Or, He was depressed by the dark, dreary weather.

One can also shorten descriptive phrases by eliminating repetitions.

> The professor assigned a paper of five pages or six pages.
> The professor assigned a five- or six-page paper.

Exercise 3-6

Rewrite the wordy descriptions in the following sentences.

1. People who are uninformed tend to vote for candidates who are well-known.
2. Joan won the competition with a performance that was brilliant.
3. He wore a coat of many colors.
4. She wore a shirt that was colorful.
5. The director is planning a movie that will last two hours or three hours.
6. He saved money for graduate school by only buying books that were used.
7. Frank liked the song that was soft and beautiful.
8. Carrie had two children who were polite and well behaved.
9. I am looking for a job that will satisfy me more.

10. With a look that told of her deep sadness, Debbie turned and walked away.
11. The problems of teenagers are often overwhelming.
12. The teacher liked his paper on French music.
13. The teacher liked the paper of John's.
14. The car that Leslie owns is red.
15. The house that belongs to John is for sale.

Answers

1. Uninformed people tend to vote for well-known candidates. (I hope you caught both of the problems in this example.)
2. Joan won the competition with a brilliant performance.
3. He wore a many-colored coat.
4. She wore a colorful dress.
5. The director is planning a two- or three-hour movie.
6. He saved money for graduate school by only buying used books.
7. Frank liked the soft, beautiful song.
8. Carrie had two polite, well-behaved children.
9. I am looking for a more satisfying job.
10. With a deeply sad look, Debbie turned and walked away.
11. Teenagers' problems are often overwhelming.
12. Correct. (A shorter version would probably be ambiguous.)
13. The teacher liked John's paper.
14. Leslie's car is red.
15. John's house is for sale.

You might prefer the original version of sentence 10 if you were writing fiction. However, in expository writing, succinctness is more important than flowery language. As has been stated above, in nonfiction, the shorter version is not always the preferable one, but it usually is. Did you catch the rewriting mistake in sentence 4?

Pointers
1. Rewrite long, descriptive phrases.
2. Consider how editing will affect the meaning, variety, and flow of your paper. Don't change something if it changes the meaning.

Eliminate Wordy Negative Expressions

Another way to pare wordiness, as well as make your writing sound more direct, is to express the negative in a positive form. Similarly, a writer should try to avoid statements that use the word *not*.

> Max is not trustworthy.
> Max is untrustworthy.

> She could not remember his name.
> She forgot his name.

> That argument is not important.
> That argument is trifling (or unimportant).

Exercise 3-7

Edit the following sentences to eliminate the wordy negative expressions.

1. Marge is not going to the prom.
2. The child doesn't like carrots.
3. Jane was not encouraged by her grade in French.
4. The teacher doesn't trust Bob's honesty.
5. Her coat wasn't very big.
6. The child was not afraid of the bully.

7. Susan was not intimidated by the steep slope.
8. The accident occurred because Laura did not pay attention to her parent's rules.
9. The change in the law is not major.
10. The professor does not frequently give Fs.

Answers
1. Marge is skipping the prom.
2. The child dislikes carrots.
3. Jane was discouraged by her French grade.
4. The teacher distrusts Bob.
5. Her coat was small.
6. The child was unafraid of the bully.
7. Susan was unintimidated by the steep slope.
8. The accident occurred because Laura ignored her parent's rules.
9. The change in the law is minor.
10. The professor gives Fs infrequently.

Note that eliminating wordy negative expressions can also help you avoid ambiguity. In particular, double negatives are confusing.

Pointers

1. Eliminate wordy negative expressions.
2. Avoid double negatives, which cause ambiguity.

Shorten Introductory Phrases

One can often shorten introductory phrases by replacing a noun and a verb with the "-ing" form of the verb.

> After she ate diner, Marcia went to bed.
> After eating dinner, Marcia went to bed.

The first version is not incorrect; a writer can use both constructions for variety.

Exercise 3-8

Change the nouns and verbs in the introductory clauses to the "-ing" form of the verbs.

1. While he was on vacation, Doug visited his sister in Denver.
2. After she waited for three years, Sarah applied to law school.
3. Before you brush your teeth, you should gargle with a mouthwash.
4. When you cook Chinese food, you should chop the vegetables finely.
5. When you look at the sky, you should be careful not to stare directly at the sun.

Answers
1. While vacationing, Doug visited his sister.
2. After waiting three years, Sarah applied to law school.
3. Before brushing, you should gargle with a mouthwash.
4. When cooking Chinese food, you should chop the vegetables finely.
5. When looking at the sky, you should be careful not to stare directly at the sun.

When making the above changes, be careful not to create a dangling participle—a phrase that attaches to the wrong subject.

Exercise 3-9

Eliminate the wordiness in the following sentences using the techniques contained in this chapter.

1. Each and every person should work for charities for free.
2. Owing to the fact that weather here in the city of Daytona usually is warm in the winter, it is probable that heating costs will be low.
3. There are several factors to be considered, such as the time of year, the weather, and so on.
4. It is obvious that one must study a number of hours per day to succeed in law school.
5. There are at least five people who can do the job as well as Bob can do the job.
6. He stared at Bob's hair, which is red in color.
7. The teacher talked to John's parents in regard to a number of problems he was having with his schoolwork.
8. Marie wanted to attend Columbia University, which is in the city of New York, owing to the fact that it is highly regarded reputation-wise.
9. Kate is a person who will be a good social worker based on the fact that she cares about people.
10. It is obvious that the economy will not improve until the time that consumers begin to spend more money or until the time that Congress reduces taxes.
11. He liked the stories of John Cheever.
12. Becky married Sam because he is kind and because he is handsome.
13. The plays are in two acts or in three acts.
14. Owing to the fact that it was snowing and owing to the fact that it was cold, Bob wore his heavy coat, and Bob wore his earmuffs.
15. John walked down the road in a slow manner, due to the fact that he had hurt his foot in an accident that was nobody's fault.
16. She is a player who can have an impact on the team's rebounding.
17. In spite of the fact he was tired, Larry went to the party.
18. The review was pertaining to the book of Mary Davis.
19. Jack is a person who likes clothes that are blue in color.

20. Each and every guest will receive a prize.

Answers

1. Everyone should work for charities.
2. Because the weather in Daytona is usually warm in the winter, heating costs will probably be low.
3. We must consider several factors, such as the time of the year and the weather.
4. One must study several hours per day to succeed in law school.
5. At least five people can do the job as well as Bob can.
6. He stared at Bob's red hair.
7. The teacher talked to John's parents about problems he was having with his schoolwork.
8. Maria wanted to attend Columbia University in New York City because it is highly regarded.
9. Kate will be a good social worker because she cares about people.
10. The economy will not improve until consumers begin to spend more money or Congress reduces taxes.
11. He liked John Cheever's stories.
12. Becky married John because he is kind and handsome.
13. The plays are in two or three acts.
14. Because it was snowing and cold, Bob wore his heavy coat and earmuffs.
15. John walked down the road slowly because he had accidentally hurt his foot.
16. She can help the team's rebounding.
17. Although he was tired, Larry went to the party.
18. The review was about Mary Davis's book.
19. Jack likes blue clothes.
20. Each guest will receive a prize.

Did you recognize the sentences with multiple problems? Did you catch any rewriting mistakes?

Exercise 3-10

Look for wordiness in a paper you have recently written. Repeat this exercise until you are proficient at spotting wordiness.

Exercise 3-11

Edit the following paragraph using the techniques you have studied in this book.

> It is obvious that the defendant is guilty of the crime of murder he is accused of. First, a number of witnesses saw him run from the scene of the crime in a quick manner. Second, his fingerprints were found on the gun that was used for the murder by the police. Third, tests showed that he had recently fired a gun within the last six hours. Finally, he could not produce an alibi that showed he was elsewhere at the time the murder was committed. Based on these facts, the defendant should receive a conviction from the jury.

Answer

> The defendant is obviously guilty of murder. First, several witnesses saw him run from the crime scene. Second, the police found his prints on the murder weapon. Third, tests showed that he had fired a gun within the last six hours. Finally, he could not produce an alibi. Accordingly, the jury should convict the defendant.

Did you recognize the sentences using passive voice?

Conclusion

The chapter has shown how to improve your writing by recognizing and correcting mechanical problems (wordiness) in your drafts. The key to fixing these problems is awareness; once you are aware that your writing contains wordiness, the problem is easy to correct. The best way to recognize these problems is to read your drafts out loud. While each unnecessary word may seem minor, if you can correct all the minor problems in your papers, your writing will markedly improve.

As I mentioned earlier, when I started to look for wordiness in my papers, I found that I could eliminate about one in ten pages just by eliminating wordiness.

Chapter 4

Emphasis, Clarity, and Specificity

Chapter Goals

1. To help you start thinking about other aspects of your writing, such as emphasis, clarity, and specificity.
2. To show you how to emphasize important ideas and de-emphasize less important ones in sentences.
3. To show you how to use placement to create emphasis and subordination in sentences.
4. To show you how to use sentence structure to create emphasis and subordination in sentences.
5. To show you how to use punctuation to create emphasis and subordination in sentences.
6. To show you how to create clarity by making clear lists.
7. To help you avoid clichés and legal jargon.
8. To help you be specific; to help you write exactly what you intend.
9. To make you aware of the meaning of every word you write.

Emphasis

Everything in writing is not equally important. An effective writer emphasizes important ideas and subordinates secondary ones. Methods that a writer can use to emphasize or de-emphasize include placement, sentence structure, and punctuation. This chapter will deal with emphasis in sentences; Chapters 5 and 6 treat emphasis in paragraphs.

Placement of words or ideas in a sentence affects emphasis. Words at the beginning and end of a sentence receive the most emphasis; words in the middle the least. Consider the following examples.

> Lee Harvey Oswald, who was killed by Jack Ruby, assassinated President Kennedy.
>
> The man who was killed by Jack Ruby, Lee Harvey Oswald, assassinated President Kennedy.
>
> Jack Ruby killed the man who assassinated President Kennedy, Lee Harvey Oswald.
>
> Jack Ruby killed Lee Harvey Oswald, who assassinated President Kennedy.
>
> President Kennedy was assassinated by Lee Harvey Oswald, who was killed by Jack Ruby.
>
> President Kennedy was assassinated by the man killed by Jack Ruby, Lee Harvey Oswald.

Each of these examples says the same thing, but each emphasizes a different noun. For example, in the first sentence, Lee Harvey Oswald is emphasized by placement at the beginning of the sentence. Jack Ruby receives the least emphasis because of placement in the middle of the sentence. With the possible exception of the passive sentences, no sentence is preferable. Rather, the writer should use the sentence that provides the emphasis he or she desires.

Exercise 4-1

Rewrite the following sentences to change the emphasis. Consider varying the normal pattern of a simple sentence (object-verb-noun rather than noun-verb-object) and using passive voice for emphasis.

1. Bill, Ann Smith's son, attends Harvard.
2. Larry won the lottery.

3. Analysis is the most important part of your law exam grade.
4. The spectacular sunset awed the tourists.
5. Three congressman, including Senator Sanchez, visited the accident site.
6. Pilot error caused the plane crash.
7. Jane, a student in Dr. Wong's class, won the essay contest.
8. Many Americans' favorite sport is baseball.
9. The volcano spewed forth lava.
10. The judge sentenced the criminal.
11. She spent two hours finding the error in the computer program.
12. The criminal confirmed that he had murdered Martin by the actions he took the next day.
13. Marge marked the calendar to remember her father's birthday.
14. John's sheepish grin showed that he was embarrassed by Bill's story.

Answers

1. Ann Smith's son, Bill, attends Harvard. (If the story is about Bill, the original version of the sentence is preferable. If the story is about Ann, the latter version is probably preferable.)
2. The lottery was won by Larry. (The writer has emphasized the lottery.)
3. The most important part of your law exam grade is analysis.
4. The tourists stared at the spectacular sunset.
5. Senator Sanchez, along with two other congressmen, visited the accident site.
6. Investigators revealed that pilot error caused the plane crash.
7. Dr. Wong's student, Jane, won the essay contest.
8. Baseball is the favorite sport of many Americans.
9. Lava spewed from the volcano.
10. The criminal received his sentence from the judge.
11. Finding the error in the computer program took her two hours.
12. The actions the criminal took the next day confirmed that he had murdered Martin.
13. To remember her father's birthday, Marge marked the calendar.
14. That John was embarrassed by Bill's story was shown by his sheepish grin.

Can you see how placement affects the emphasis in the examples you wrote? Can you see why this is important? While the exercises in this section are generally easy, it is important that you recognize the possibilities so that you can use them in your writing.

Exercise 4-2

Find a newspaper article, and mark the words in each sentence that receive the most emphasis. Rewrite the sentences to change the emphasis.

Sentence structure can affect emphasis. An idea in an independent clause usually receives more stress than an idea in a dependent clause.[1] Compare the following examples.

> Although Max had dreamed of becoming a doctor [dependent clause], he held menial jobs most of his life [independent clause].
>
> Max had dreamed of becoming a doctor [independent clause], but he held menial jobs most of his life [dependent clause].

The first sentence emphasizes that Max had held menial jobs; the second sentence that Max had dreamed of becoming a doctor.

The order of the clauses can also affect emphasis. Compare the above examples with the following.

> Max held menial jobs for most of his life, although he had dreamed of becoming a doctor.
>
> Although Max held menial jobs for most of his life, he had dreamed of becoming a doctor.
>
> For most of his life, Max held menial jobs, although he had dreamed of becoming a doctor.
>
> Although Max had dreamed of becoming a doctor, for most of his life, he held menial jobs.

---

1. An independent clause can stand alone as a sentence. A dependent clause can't. I will discuss independent and dependent clauses in more detail in the next chapter.

The above sentences say the same thing, and, for the most part, they sound equally correct. The version one chooses depends on the emphasis desired (and how the sentence fits with other sentences in the paragraph). You should never settle for the first version but should consider all correct means of expression. Of course, you should also make sure that the words, phrases, and clauses of a sentence are in a logical order, that the sentence is easily comprehensible, and that it says what you intend.

Exercise 4-3

Rewrite the following sentence in as many ways as possible.

> Although he loved Laura, Bill complied with his mother's wishes and married Joanne, his mother's protégée.

Answers
1. Bill complied with his mother's wishes and married Joanne, his mother's protégée, although he loved Laura.
2. Bill complied with his mother's wishes and married his mother's protégée, Joanne, although he loved Laura.
3. Bill married Joanne, his mother's protégée, to comply with his mother's wishes, although he loved Laura.

Punctuation can also affect emphasis, especially punctuation of descriptions or parenthetical expressions. Consider the following examples.

> Bill married Laura—his mother's protégée.
> Bill married Laura, his mother's protégée.
> Bill married Laura (his mother's protégée).

"His mother's protégée" is strongly emphasized in the first sentence, it receives normal emphasis in the second sentence, and it is de-emphasized in the last sentence. Say each of these sentences out loud, giving them the emphasis indicated by the punctuation. Most writers will generally use a comma to set off descriptions. However, carefully considering whether you should emphasize or de-emphasize a description can improve the effectiveness of your writing.

Exercise 4-4

Rewrite the following sentences to add emphasis; then subtract emphasis.

1. George Smith, the president of Smith University, spoke at our graduation.
2. *Aida*, an opera set in ancient Egypt, is Betty's favorite piece of music.
3. His favorite team, the Cardinals, won the tournament.
4. He was dating Angela, Bill's sister.
5. She visited Niagara Falls, the most beautiful waterfall in the world, then she went to Toronto.

Answers

1. George Smith—the president of Smith University—spoke at our graduation.
   George Smith (the president of Smith University) spoke at our graduation.
2. *Aida*—an opera set in ancient Egypt—is Betty's favorite piece of music.
   Aida (an opera set in ancient Egypt) is Betty's favorite opera.
3. His favorite team—the Cardinals—won the tournament.
   His favorite team (the Cardinals) won the tournament.
4. He was dating Angela—Bill's sister.
   He was dating Angela (Bill's sister).
5. She visited Niagara Falls—the most beautiful waterfall in the world, then she went to Toronto.
   She visited Niagara Falls (the most beautiful waterfall in the world), then she went to Toronto.

Note the punctuation in sentence 5. A dash does not replace the second comma in version one because the comma is needed to punctuate the independent clauses. Similarly, both the closing parentheses and comma are required in version two.

One can also create emphasis by underlining important passages or by using special fonts or typefaces. However, you should not overuse these techniques.

> The court held that there is **no** instance where estoppel can be used against the government.

> The court held that there is no instance where estoppel can be used against the government, except in cases involving IRS opinion letters.

The emphasis techniques used above apply to all types of writing. However, they are particularly important in legal writing because legal writers often create persuasive documents. You can use all these devices to create emphasis or to de-emphasize something. For example, placement within a sentence is important for persuasive writing. Similarly, by putting an idea in an independent clause, you emphasize it, while if you put it in a dependent clause, you de-emphasize it.

> John Smith robbed the store.
> The store was robbed.

John Smith is de-emphasized in the second sentence by the use of the passive.

> The contract had not been signed by the company's president. It had been signed by its CFO.
> Although the contract had not been signed by the company's president, it was signed by its CFO.

In the second sentence, the fact that the company president had not signed the contract is de-emphasized by placing it in a dependent clause. As you read it, notice how your attention is focused on the independent clause.

> The contract was signed by the company's CFO, although it had not been signed by its president.

This version further de-emphasizes the fact that the contract was not signed by the company's president by placing the idea at the end of the sentence.

> Although there was no moon on the night of the robbery, there was a street lamp nearby.
> On the night of the robbery, there was a street lamp nearby, although there was no moon.
> There was no moon on the night of the robbery, although there was a street lamp nearby.

Can you see how each version emphasizes and de-emphasizes certain ideas?

> Jack Chin, a career criminal, was arrested for speeding at Oak and Main Streets about five minutes after the robbery.
> Jack Chin—a career criminal—was arrested for speeding at Oak and Main Streets about five minutes after the robbery.
> Jack Chin (a career criminal) was arrested for speeding at Oak and Main Streets about five minutes after the robbery.

The changes in the punctuation in these sentences make a big difference in how you read them. In sentence two, the writer emphasizes that Jack Chin is a career criminal. Do you know why I used passive voice for these sentences?

Make Lists Clear

A writer can make a list clearer by using numbers or letters to mark off items. Compare the following sentences.

> The study examined four groups: boys aged 14–18, girls aged 14–18, men aged 24–28, and women aged 24–28.
>
> The study examined four groups: (1) boys aged 14–18, (2) girls aged 14–18, (3) men aged 24–28, and (4) women aged 24–28.

The second sentence is easier to read, and the reader is more likely to remember it.

Exercise 4-5

Separate the items in the following lists with numbers or letters.

1. The study concluded that the major causes of legal malpractice suits are missed deadlines, conflicts of interest, and failure to communicate with the client.

2. The investigator told us that there were three possible causes of the accident: the plaintiff was driving too fast, the defendant was fighting with his wife and failed to see the plaintiff's car, or the steering on the defendant's car was defective.

3. Critics attack the conclusions of the Warren Commission on the following grounds: the Zapruder film shows that Kennedy was shot from the front, doctors at Parkland hospital have testified that there was an exit wound on the back of Kennedy's head, numerous witnesses heard shots from the Grassy Knoll, and paraffin tests demonstrated that Oswald had not fired a rifle on November 22.

4. Critics believe that four groups might have been involved in the Kennedy assassination: the CIA, the Mafia, anti-Castro Cubans, and right-wing oilmen.

5. Barbara's doctoral orals will involve four areas: 19th-century architecture, Baroque painting, Bernini, and aesthetics.

Answers

1. The study concluded that the major causes of legal malpractice are (1) missed deadlines, (2) conflicts of interest, and (3) failure to communicate with the client.

2. The investigator told us that there were three possible causes of the accident:

   1. the plaintiff was driving too fast,
   2. the defendant was fighting with his wife and failed to see the plaintiff's car, or
   3. the steering on the defendant's car was defective.

3. Critics attack the conclusions of the Warren Commission on the following grounds:

   a. the Zapruder film shows that Kennedy was shot from the front;
   b. doctors at Parkland Hospital have testified that there was an exit wound on the back of Kennedy's head;
   c. numerous witnesses heard shots from the Grassy Knoll; and
   d. paraffin tests demonstrated that Oswald had not fired a rifle on November 22.

4. Critics believe that four groups might have been involved in the Kennedy assassination: (1) the CIA, (2) the Mafia, (3) anti-Castro Cubans, and (4) right-wing oilmen.
5. Barbara's doctoral orals will involve four areas: (1) 19th-century architecture, (2) Baroque painting, (3) Bernini, and (4) aesthetics.

Of course, you can overdo the above; you should not number every list. When using a list make sure that all items are parallel.

> Incorrect: John has three hobbies: (1) fishing, (2) he likes to go to the movies, and (3) to build model airplane kits.
> Correct: John has three hobbies: (1) fishing, (2) going to the movies, and (3) building model airplane kits.

Pointers

1. Make lists clearer by numbering the individual factors.
2. Make sure that lists are parallel.

Avoid Clichés and Legal Jargon

Clichés subtract from the effect of your writing. Avoid them whenever possible.

> We will litigate this action to the bitter end. (the bitter end)
> Making this argument would be entering into dangerous waters. (dangerous waters)
> Courts have been in a tug-of-war over this issue. (tug-of-war)
> This lawsuit reopens the old debate over the purpose of tort law. (old debate)

Similarly, legal jargon makes writing unclear and pompous.

> The defendant shall cease and desist from the illegal activities.
> The defendant shall cease the illegal activities.

> The party of the first part shall pay the party of the second part five hundred dollars.
> John Jones shall pay Joan Smith five hundred dollars.

> The jury found said defendant guilty.
> The jury found the defendant guilty.

Avoid the following lawyerisms whenever possible: aforesaid, aforementioned, said, heretofore, hereinafter, party of the first part, cease and desist, null and void, each and every, force and effect, save and except, full and complete, unless and until, and so on.

Of course, you do not have to avoid words that have become legal terms of art, such as fee simple absolute, res judicata, offer, and consideration.

Exercise 4-6

1. The engineer's testimony is a circumstance over which we have no control.
2. If worse comes to worse, we can always argue that the plaintiff should recover for unjust enrichment.
3. It goes without saying that the plaintiff's argument will fail.
4. This argument is contrary to the cherished belief that negligence victims should recover from tortfessors.
5. This argument is a mirror to the one the defendant made in *Smith v. Jones*.
6. The defendants shall cease and desist occupancy of said premises immediately.
7. The plaintiff established negligence by res ipsa loquitur.

8. Upon completion of construction of the annex, the party of the first part shall notify the party of the second part.
9. If either party breaches this agreement, all duties hereunder shall be null and void.
10. The court dismissed the claim based on res judicata.

Answers

1. We cannot control the engineer's testimony.
2. If these arguments fail, we can argue that the plaintiff should recover for unjust enrichment.
3. The plaintiff's argument will fail.
4. This argument is contrary to the principle that negligence victims should recover from tortfessors.
5. This argument is similar to [or mirrors] the one the defendant made in *Smith v. Jones.*
6. The defendants shall vacate the premises immediately.
7. Correct. Res ipsa loquitur is a legal term of art.
8. When the annex is completed, Jones Construction shall notify the school board. (Did you catch the other problem in this sentence?)
9. If either party breaches this agreement, all duties under this agreement shall be terminated.
10. Correct.

Pointer

Eliminate clichés and legal jargon from your writing.

Be Specific

A thesaurus is full of words with similar meanings. However, if you examine each synonym carefully, you will find that few words mean exactly the same thing; there are usually nuances of meaning between synonyms.

One of the keys to effective writing is to use words that convey the precise meaning you intend. This is especially true for lawyers. The use of one word may be the difference between winning and losing a case.

For example, imagine you are defending a disability discrimination case. The key issue is whether the plaintiff is disabled under the applicable statute. What word do you use for the plaintiff's alleged disability? If you use the word "disability" or "handicap," you are conceding the plaintiff's case. "Impairment" is better, but "condition" is probably best. "Condition" lacks the unfavorable connotations of "disability," "handicap," and "impairment."

Exercise 4-7

Replace the general verbs in the following sentences with specific ones.

1. The child ran down the street.
2. The angry man looked at the noisy child.
3. Jane spoke softly to her baby.
4. Carl looked over the report.
5. David drank the wine.
6. Peggy let go of the glass.
7. The airplane flew through the clouds.
8. The professor spoke the lecture in a monotonous tone.
9. The lovers walked through the garden.
10. The dog ate the steak.

Answers
1. The child raced down the street.
2. The angry man glared at the noisy child.
3. Jane whispered to her baby.

4. Carl scanned the report.
5. David sipped the wine.
6. Peggy dropped the glass.
7. The airplane soared through the clouds.
8. The professor droned the lecture.
9. The lovers strolled through the garden.
10. The dog devoured the steak.

Being specific applies to every word and phrase in the sentence. When you add an adjective or adverb to a sentence, be as precise as possible. Similarly, prepositional phrases can help make sentences more specific. They often indicate when or where an action took place.

Exercise 4-8

Make the following sentences as specific as possible.

1. The man went to the zoo with the child.
2. Jack made a painting for class.
3. Marge ate her lunch.
4. They went to a concert.
5. Nellie was sick recently.
6. They treated the dog badly.
7. The elephant made a loud sound.
8. Mark went shopping.
9. He liked sports.
10. He wore a nice suit.

Answers
1. The old man visited the Louisville Zoo with his youngest grandchild.
2. Jack painted a landscape for art class.
3. Marge hungrily devoured the hero sandwich.
4. The young couple attended Richter's sold-out recital.
5. Nellie missed work on Thursday because she had the swine flu.

6. The children mistreated the dog by pulling her ears.
7. The old elephant bellowed.
8. Mark shopped at the mall for clothes and records.
9. Vlad likes to watch baseball and golf.
10. He wore a conservative, gray suit.

As you read the above, notice how the specific examples convey much more meaning than the original ones. Effective writing depends on the use of detail.

Some adjectives point (demonstrative adjectives—that man, these people, such people), while others (articles) merely fill space. Compare the following examples.

The man murdered his wife.
That man murdered his wife.

I want the apples.
I want those apples.

The school will not tolerate the behavior.
This school will not tolerate such behavior.

Whether the writer uses demonstrative adjectives or articles depends on the writer's goals in a particular context. However, a writer should not develop lazy habits and use articles when demonstrative adjectives will work better.

Exercise 4-9

Replace the articles in the following sentences with demonstrative adjectives.

1. Walter drove the car.
2. The shopper wanted the apples and oranges.
3. I dislike the dress over there.
4. The man appears suspicious.
5. The nations endorsed the plan.

6. The charity appreciates the efforts.
7. The paper will discuss recent developments in copyright law.
8. Wally wore a dress to the Halloween party.
9. Jack painted a landscape for art class.
10. The young couple is headed for trouble.

Answers

1. Walter drove that car.
2. That shopper wanted those apples and these oranges.
3. I dislike that dress. (Notice how the use of a demonstrative adjective saved words.)
4. That man appears suspicious.
5. These nations endorsed this plan.
6. The charity appreciates such efforts.
7. This paper will discuss recent developments in copyright law.
8. Wally wore that dress to the Halloween party.
9. Jack painted this landscape for art class.
10. That young couple is headed for trouble.

As with most of the techniques I discuss in this book, you shouldn't overuse demonstrative adjectives.

Of course, demonstrative adjectives are not the only way to make nouns more specific. Personal pronouns, possessives, and adjectives can make a general description into a specific one.

I liked the dress.
I liked that dress.
I liked her dress.
I liked Brenda's dress.
I liked the red dress.
I liked Brenda's new, red dress.

Exercise 4-10

Make the nouns in the following sentences more specific by using demonstrative adjectives, adjectives, possessives, prepositional phrases, dependent clauses, or personal pronouns.

1. I went to the park.
2. John wore a new suit.
3. Nan likes to read magazines.
4. Juan likes to watch sports.
5. The man watched the children.
6. Mary wants to buy a car.
7. The judge read the decision.
8. The lawyer questioned the witness.
9. The winter was long and cold.
10. The batter hit a home run.

Answers
1. I drove to the new city park by the river.
2. John wore a brown suit that he bought at the mall yesterday.
3. Nan likes to read travel magazines.
4. Juan likes to watch winter sports.
5. The old man watched the neighborhood children who were playing ball in the park.
6. Mary wants to buy a new American car.
7. The old judge read his decision.
8. The plaintiff's lawyer questioned the reluctant witness.
9. Last winter was long and cold.
10. Reggie Jackson hit a home run into the upper deck in right field.

A writer can destroy specificity by using qualifiers. Consider the following examples.

> Jack is rather handsome.
> Carol's writing is the most unique I have ever read.

This steak is so good.

Are the words *rather*, *most*, and *so* in the above sentences necessary? *Rather* adds nothing to handsome, but it makes the writer sound like she is hedging. The second sentence is incorrect; there are no degrees of unique. *So good* sounds strange.

Exercise 4-11

Eliminate the qualifiers in the following sentences.

1. Mike was pretty disgusted with his grade.
2. Martha was rather angry at her boyfriend.
3. I am fairly sure that the Pirates will win their division.
4. The new student seems a little strange.
5. Klimt's painting style is very unique.
6. Pat thought the exercise was kind of dumb.
7. These exercises are very worthwhile.
8. Carl thought that the new student was sort of nice.
9. The explosion occurred quite recently.
10. Professor Smith keeps very current on contract law.

Answers
1. Mike was disgusted with his grade.
2. Martha was angry at her boyfriend.
3. I am sure the Yankees will win their division.
4. The new student seems strange.
5. Klimt's painting style is unique.
6. Pat thought the exercise was dumb.
7. These exercises are worthwhile.
8. Carl thought that the new student was nice.
9. The explosion occurred recently.
10. Professor Smith keeps current on contract law.

(Did you catch the rewriting change in sentence 3?)

As was true of the techniques discussed earlier in this chapter, word choice is particularly important in persuasive writing. Some words that have the same meaning can have very different emotional connotations. You should always carefully consider the emotional connotations of your word choice.

> Agent Booth pushed the defendant against the wall.
> Agent Booth slammed the defendant against the wall.

> Juan cried out when he was hit by the foul ball.
> Juan screamed when he was hit by the foul ball.

> Molly crashed into the other car.
> Molly hit the other car.

As you can see in the above examples, you can use word choice both for emphasis and de-emphasis. Of course, you need to make sure the word you have chosen is accurate. You can't say "Molly slammed into the other car" when she barely tapped it.

Caveat: Be careful when using persuasive devices in your writing. It is easy to overdo it. Always use persuasive devices in context. Develop an ear for what is proper. A fact statement in a torts case may permit more persuasion than an argument section of a brief in a corporations case.

Exercise 4-12

Improve the persuasiveness of the following sentences through word choice.

1. The robber gave the note to the teller.
2. After the argument, Bob left the house.
3. Homer ate the meatloaf.
4. Travis pushed Shirley out of the way.
5. Wanda turned around when the police car approached.
6. The defendant broke the window.

7. Corey ran up the stairs.
8. The dog barked at the intruder.
9. The driver drove away after the bank robbery.
10. Nathan looked at the suspect.

Answers

1. The robber thrust the note at the teller.
2. After the argument, Bob stormed out of the house.
3. Homer devoured the meatloaf.
4. Travis shoved Shirley out of the way.
5. Wanda spun around when the police car approached.
6. The defendant smashed the window.
7. Corey dashed up the stairs.
8. The dog growled at the intruder.
9. The driver sped away after the bank robbery.
10. Nathan glared at the suspect.

Pointers

1. Always use the exact word that conveys the meaning you intend. Being specific is usually better than being general. A lawyer does not want to be vague when making arguments, and details win cases.
2. Think about how specific types of words or phrases, adjectives, adverbs, and prepositional phrases can help make your writing more precise.
3. Avoid unnecessary qualifiers.
4. Use word choice in persuasive writing. Consider the emotional connotation of every word you write.

Exercise 4-13

Edit the following paragraph using the techniques presented in this and earlier chapters.

It is obvious that the Court does not have personal jurisdiction over Smith, Inc. Smith, Inc., a Delaware corporation, does not have minimum contacts with the state of Kentucky. Smith, Inc., is not licensed to do business in Kentucky, and it does not do any business here in the state. Having jurisdiction over Smith, Inc., by this Court would be quite unfair, and it would be against the concept of due process. Consequently, dismissal of the complaint should be made by the Court.

Answer

This Court cannot assert personal jurisdiction over Smith, Inc.—a Delaware corporation—because it lacks minimum contacts with Kentucky. Smith, Inc., is not licensed to do business in Kentucky, and it does no business here. This Court's assertion of jurisdiction over Smith, Inc., would be unfair and violate due process. Consequently, this Court should dismiss the plaintiff's complaint.

Exercise 4-14

1. Look through a legal document you recently wrote. Did you use emphasis techniques to help your reader see what was important and not important? Did you use placement in the sentence to create emphasis? Did you use sentence structure to create emphasis? Did you place ideas in independent and dependent clauses to create emphasis? Did you use punctuation to create emphasis? Did you consider every word you wrote to see if it conveyed the proper meaning?
2. Look through a persuasive document you recently wrote. How did you create persuasiveness in the document? Did you use placement to create persuasiveness? Did you use sentence structure to create persuasiveness? Did you use word choice to create persuasiveness? How did you de-emphasize material? Is the persuasiveness subtle, or did you overdo it? How would a judge react to the persuasiveness in your document?

Conclusion

I hope that you are now looking at your writing in a different way based on what you have learned in this chapter. A writer doesn't just want to get his ideas on paper; he should want to express the exact ideas that are in his head to the reader with the proper emphasis.

Chapter 5

Combining Sentences and Editing Paragraphs

Chapter Goals

1. To help you understand the different types of sentence patterns so that you can learn how to use them.
2. To show you how to combine sentences for variety, coherence, and flow.
3. To make you aware of redundant sentences.
4. To help you recognize empty sentences.
5. To help you avoid overusing a particular word within a paragraph.
6. To help you recognize and avoid abrupt changes of verb tense.
7. To help you to consider the paragraph level, not just the word and sentence levels.
8. To help you develop your "ear" for flow within and between sentences.

Consider the following paragraphs:

Martin Smith argued the appellant's case in front of the court. Smith is a Harvard professor. He contended that the police's actions constituted an illegal search under the 4th Amendment. He contended that this illegal search made all evidence found during the search inadmissible at trial. Smith argued eloquently. However, the court upheld the lower court's decision. It did so based on *Rodgers v. State*. This case had recently been decided by the Supreme Court. It held that a similar search was constitutional. It was constitutional because the defendant's rights were protected.

Martin Smith, a Harvard professor, argued the appellant's case before the court. He contended that the police's actions constituted an illegal search under the 4th Amendment and that this illegal search made all evidence found during the search inadmissible at trial. Although Smith argued eloquently, the court upheld the lower court's decision based on *Rodgers v. State*, which the Supreme Court had recently decided. That case held that a similar search was constitutional because the defendant's rights were protected.

The first version seems choppy; the second version reads much better because short sentences are combined and there is greater variety in sentence structure. This chapter will examine sentence types and how to combine sentences, as well as other aspects of editing paragraphs.

Recognizing Sentence Patterns and Combining Sentences

Many sentence patterns exist in the English language, ranging from simple sentences to complex sentences with several dependent clauses. A simple sentence consists of a noun and a verb with or without additional modifying words and a direct and/or indirect object.

> John laughed.
> John laughed loudly.
> Jackie went to the store.
> Martin wore a red shirt to the party.
> Alberto gave him the book.

While simple sentences are common, your writing will be choppy and uninteresting if you only use short, simple sentences. Moreover, a series of simple sentences lacks flow. One way to create longer sentences is to combine two simple sentences. However, you should combine sentences only when they belong together, such as sentences that concern the same idea or when sentence two expands on sentence one.

1. Jackie went to the store. She then went to the pool.
2. Jackie went to the store; she then went to the pool.
3. Jackie went to the store and the pool.
4. Jackie went to the store, and she went to the pool.
5. After Jackie went to the store, she went to the pool.
6. Jackie went to the store; afterwards, she went to the pool.
7. Sam ate dinner; he left for college the next week. (Incorrect. The two ideas in the independent clauses obviously do not belong together.)
8. The Ohio court has personal jurisdiction over the Indiana defendant in this case because the defendant's act of posting defamatory information on the Internet from his Indiana home was intended to harm the plaintiff in Ohio, and the defendant has never visited Ohio. (Incorrect. The two ideas in the independent clauses obviously do not belong together.)

Versions two to six above present examples of how to combine simple sentences. Sentence two combines the sentences with a semicolon. Sentence three merges the sentences into another simple sentence. Sentence four employs a conjunction to combine the sentences. Version five converts the first sentence into a dependent clause. Version six uses a linking adverb. Which version is preferable depends on the emphasis you want and how the sentence fits with the sentences that precede and follow it. *Writing that uses a wide variety of sentence patterns is more interesting and readable than writing that relies on one or two patterns.* Sentences seven and eight are poor sentences because the ideas they contain do not go together. They are on different subjects.

One can often combine two simple sentences into one simple sentence, especially when they repeat certain words or ideas.

Laura likes Chinese food. She also likes French food.
Laura likes Chinese and French food.

Not only does sentence two combine two simple sentences, it eliminates four words without changing the meaning.

One can combine several simple sentences into one.

> Laura likes Chinese food. She also likes French food. She also likes German food.
> Laura likes Chinese, French, and German food.

You can also combine two simple sentences into compound sentences, comprising two independent clauses. Independent clauses can stand alone as a sentence.

> Larry played basketball with his friends. He then visited his grandmother.
> Larry played basketball with his friends, then he visited his grandmother.
> Larry played basketball with his friends, and he visited his grandmother.
> Larry played basketball with his friends; afterwards, he visited his grandmother.

The most common way to combine independent clauses is with conjunctions, such as "and" or "or." Always use a comma before the conjunction to avoid a run-on sentence.

> Carl backed the car out of the driveway. He drove south on Maple Street.
> Carl backed the car out of the driveway and he drove south on Maple Street. (incorrect)
> Carl backed the car out of the driveway [independent clause], and he drove south on Maple Street [independent clause]. (correct)

> We will go to the beach. If it is too hot, we will go to the movies.
> We will go to the beach but, if it is too hot, we will go to the movies. (incorrect)
> We will go to the beach, but, if it is too hot, we will go to the movies. (correct)

(Note that the last example consists of an independent clause combined with an independent clause preceded by a dependent clause.)

One can also combine two independent clauses with a conjunction and leave out the noun in the second clause, producing a simple sentence.

> Carl backed the car out of the garage. He drove south on Maple Street.
> Carl backed the car out of the driveway and drove south on Maple Street.

A writer can also combine independent clauses by using punctuation—semicolons and colons.

> Larry usually dislikes French food. He prefers hamburgers and french fries.
> Larry usually dislikes French food; he prefers hamburgers and french fries.

> Linda has but one desire in life. She dreams of one day visiting Paris.
> Linda has but one desire in life: She dreams of one day visiting Paris.

Writers use semicolons more often than colons. A colon produces a more abrupt break and is more dramatic. (Remember, I want you to think about how punctuation can emphasize or de-emphasize ideas.)

A writer can also combine independent clauses with linking adverbs, such as *yet*, *however*, or *nevertheless*. If the linking adverb comprises four letters or more, use a semicolon after the first clause and a comma after the linking adverb. Otherwise, use a comma between the clauses.

> Peggy dislikes torts. Yet she made an A in the class.
> Peggy dislikes torts, yet she made an A in the class. (correct)
> Peggy dislikes torts; yet, she made an A in the class. (incorrect)

> Doug failed the class. He had to take it again in summer school.
> Doug failed the class; therefore, he had to take it again in summer school. (correct)

Doug failed the class, therefore he had to take it again in summer school. (incorrect)

One can join simple sentences by making one of them into a dependent clause (complex sentence). A dependent clause cannot stand alone; it does not form a complete sentence.

Peggy dislikes torts. Yet she made an A in the class.
Although Peggy dislikes torts [dependent clause], she made an A in the class [independent clause].
Peggy dislikes torts [independent clause], although she made an A in the class [dependent clause].
Peggy dislikes torts. Although she made an A in the class. (incorrect)

In sentence two, "although Peggy dislikes torts" is the dependent clause; in sentence three, it is "although she made an A in the class." Neither clause can stand alone because they are dependent clauses. Both sentences say the same thing. Sentence two emphasizes the fact that Peggy made an A; sentence three, that Peggy dislikes torts. Always consider what idea you want to emphasize in the sentence.

You can place dependent clauses at the beginning, middle, or end of a sentence.

Although Albert loved Linda, he married Donna because his parents disliked Linda.
Albert married Donna (although he loved Linda) because his parents disliked Linda.
Because his parents disliked Linda, Albert married Donna, although he loved Linda.

One places subsidiary ideas in dependent or supporting clauses; main ideas, in independent clauses. Often the choice depends on the emphasis the writer desires. Other times, the importance of the clause dictates its placement. For example, one usually places descriptions in supporting clauses.

> Diane Jones argued the case before the Supreme Court. She is a law professor at Columbia.
> Diane Jones, a Columbia law professor, argued the case before the Supreme Court.

A writer can also combine sentences by deleting the noun (or preposition) from one sentence and changing the verb into its "-ing" form (participial phrase).

> Betty finished her homework. Then she watched television.
> After finishing her homework, Betty watched television.

> Mike failed tax. This delayed his graduation a semester.
> Mike failed tax, delaying his graduation a semester.

A writer can also combine three or more sentences into one.

> Professor Johnson lectured at our law school. He teaches at Harvard University. His lecture was on *Roe v. Wade*.
> Professor Johnson of Harvard University lectured on *Roe v. Wade* at our law school.

However, a writer should be careful not to create sentences that are too long or that contain unrelated ideas.

> Although the Civil War had been over for many years and most of the participants were dead, the residents of the two towns still felt great animosity toward one another and would not attend events at the other town, even though they were only five miles apart by foot and only ten miles apart by highway, because they had heard the story of the battle many times, because their parents would not let them forget the loved ones they had lost in the battle, and because of the many

incidents, such as the Hatter murder and the Jonestown fire, which had occurred since the battle.

Exercise 5-1

Identify the following sentence patterns.

1. Last night, we went to the Knicks game. The Knicks lost.
2. Last night, we went to the Knicks game. As usual, the Knicks lost.
3. Last night, we went to the Knicks game; the Knicks lost.
4. Although I brought all my good luck charms to the game, the Knicks lost last night.
5. We went to the Knicks game last night, and the Knicks lost.
6. We enjoyed the Knicks game last night even though the Knicks lost.
7. We went to the Knicks game last night, the Knicks lost.
8. We went to the Knicks game last night and, afterwards, to a bar across the street.
9. We went to a Knicks game last night; afterwards, we went to a bar across the street.
10. At the Yankees game last night, Lin caught a foul ball.
11. At the Yankees game last night, Lin caught a foul ball, and she handed it to her daughter.
12. At the Yankees game last night, Lin caught a foul ball and handed it to her daughter.
13. At the Yankees game last night, Lin caught a foul ball, and she handed it to her daughter, even though she wanted to keep it for herself.
14. Mary could not afford to go to college. Although she had saved for many years.
15. Although she had saved for many years, Mary could not afford to go college.
16. Mary could not afford to go to college, although she had saved for many years.
17. Mary had saved for many years, but she could not afford to go to college.

18. Professor Wang, who was retired from Princeton, wrote a book about World War II in the Pacific.
19. Professor Wang wrote a book about World War II in the Pacific, and he was retired from Princeton.
20. The Plaintiff has not presented facts to support his case, therefore, the court should deny Plaintiff's motion for summary judgment.

Answers

1. Two simple sentences.
2. Despite the extra material, this is still two simple sentences.
3. This is a compound sentence consisting of two independent clauses.
4. Compound sentence consisting of a dependent clause and an independent clause.
5. Compound sentence consisting of two independent clauses.
6. Complex sentence consisting of an independent clause and a dependent clause.
7. This is a run-on sentence because the parts are not properly connected.
8. Despite its length, this is a simple sentence.
9. Compound sentence consisting of two clauses connected by a linking adverb.
10. Simple sentence.
11. Compound sentence consisting of two independent clauses.
12. Simple sentence. Can you see why?
13. This is a hybrid sentence because it has two independent clauses and a dependent clauses.
14. Simple sentence. Not a sentence because it is a dependent clause.
15. Complex sentence.
16. This is still a complex sentence. I just reversed the clauses.
17. Compound sentence consisting of two independent clauses.
18. Simple sentence, despite its length.
19. Compound sentence. Out of context, the ideas in the sentence do not seem to belong together. Always check your sentences to see if the parts belong together. Do the parts concern the same idea or are they related somehow?

20. Compound sentence connected by a linking adverb. Did I use the correct punctuation?

Exercise 5-2

Combine the following sentences in four different ways.

1. Steve spent the summer in France. While in France, he studied art history.
2. Betty wrote a paper on strip mining. It won the essay contest.
3. Al wants to go to Europe this summer. However, he doesn't have the money.
4. Terry lost the case. Still, his client was happy because of the judgment's size.
5. Jerry dropped his notes during his presentation. His boss was not happy.
6. The jury found for the plaintiff. It did so based on the Smith letter.
7. Most of Betty's practice is in the field of real estate law. However, she also does some estate planning.
8. Robert's case hinges on one piece of evidence. The piece of evidence it hinges on is the Smith letter.
9. Professor Johnson is an expert on intellectual property. She is especially known for her book on the history of patents.
10. Marcia did well in torts. She made an A. However, she received a D in property.

Answers

1. While spending the summer in France, Steve studied art history.
   Steve spent the summer in France, studying art history.
   Steve spent the summer in France, and he studied art history.
   Steve spent the summer in France; while in France, he studied art history.
2. Betty wrote a paper on strip mining, which won the essay contest.
   Betty wrote a paper on strip mining; it won the essay contest.
   Betty wrote a paper on strip mining, and it won the essay contest.

The paper that Betty wrote on strip mining won the essay contest.

3. Al wants to go to Europe this summer, but he doesn't have the money.

    Al wants to go to Europe this summer; however, he doesn't have the money.

    Although Al wants to go to Europe this summer, he doesn't have the money.

    Even though he doesn't have the money, Al wants to go to Europe this summer.

4. Although Terry lost the case, his client was happy because of the judgment's size.

    Terry lost the case, still his client was happy because of the judgment's size.

    Terry lost the case, but his client was happy because of the judgment's size.

    Despite losing the case, Terry's client was happy because of the judgment's size.

5. Because Jerry dropped his notes during his presentation, his boss was not happy.

    Jerry dropped his notes during his presentation; his boss was not happy.

    Jerry dropped his notes during his presentation, and his boss was not happy.

    Jerry dropped his notes during his presentation, making his boss unhappy.

6. The jury found for the plaintiff based on the Smith letter.

    Based on the Smith letter, the jury found for the plaintiff.

    Because of the Smith letter, the jury found for the plaintiff.

    Basing its decision on the Smith letter, the jury found for the plaintiff.

7. Although most of Betty's practice is in real estate law, she also does some estate planning.

    Most of Betty's practice is in real estate law; she also does some estate planning.

    Most of Betty's practice is in real estate law; however, she also does estate planning.

    Most of Betty's practice is in real estate law, with some estate planning.

8. Robert's case hinges on one piece of evidence: the Smith letter.
   Robert's case hinges on one piece of evidence—the Smith letter.
   The Smith letter is the key to Robert's case.
   The key to Robert's case is the Smith letter.
9. Professor Johnson is an expert on intellectual property law; she is especially known for her book on the history of patents.
   Professor Johnson is an expert on intellectual property law, being especially known for her book on the history of patents.
   Professor Johnson, an expert on intellectual property law, is especially known for her book on the history of patents.
   Professor Johnson is an expert on intellectual property law, and she is especially known for her book on the history of patents.
10. Marcia did well in torts, making an A; however, she received a D in property.
    Although Marcia did well in torts (she made an A), she received a D in property.
    Marcia did well in torts—an A, but she received a D in property.
    Even though Marcia received a D in property, she did well in torts, making an A.

(Did you catch the punctuation mistake I made in exercise four, sentence two? [; still,])

Read the ten answers above out loud. Note how the various versions emphasize a different thing. Also, note how punctuation affects the lengths of pauses and whether your voice rises or falls.

Exercise 5-3

Combine the following sentences.

1. I went to a party last night. The party was at Jane's house. I went with Monica. Monica is my closest friend.
2. The president nominated Bob Smith to the Supreme Court. Bob Smith is a conservative. He is also an anti-abortionist.

3. Last night we rented *Other People's Money*. It stars Danny Devito. He is my favorite movie star.

4. Chess is my favorite game. I like it because of the strategy. Chess is an ancient game.

5. I wanted to go to the ball game. However, Mary wanted to go to the concert. We went to the concert.

6. The weather was hot. The air conditioner was broken. It was a typical summer.

7. Frank Lloyd Wright designed many famous buildings. He designed the Guggenheim Museum and Falling Waters. He is also known for having invented the "Prairie Style."

8. St. Peter's is the most famous church in the world. It was designed by many famous architects including Bernini and Michelangelo. It was placed over St. Peter's grave.

9. Most law students want a well-paying job when they graduate. However, Martha wants a job in which she can protect the environment. Martha has loved nature since she was a child.

10. The judge felt great sympathy for the defendant. Nevertheless, he ruled for the plaintiff. The contract was clear and unambiguous.

Answers

1. Last night, I went to a party at Jane's house with Monica, my closest friend.

2. The president nominated Bob Smith, a conservative and anti-abortionist, to the Supreme Court.

3. Last night we rented *Other People's Money*, starring Danny Devito—my favorite movie star.

4. Chess, an ancient game, is my favorite game because of the strategy.

5. Although I wanted to go to the ball game, Mary wanted to go to the concert, so we went to the concert.

6. The weather was hot, and the air conditioner was broken: It was a typical summer.

7. Frank Lloyd Wright designed many famous buildings, including the Guggenheim Museum and Falling Waters; he is also known for having invented the "Prairie Style."

8. St. Peter's, the most famous church in the world, was placed over St. Peter's grave, and it was designed by many famous architects, including Bernini and Michelangelo.

9. Although most law students want well-paying jobs when they graduate, Martha, who has loved nature since she was a child, wants a job in which she can protect the environment.

10. The judge felt great sympathy for the defendant; nevertheless, he ruled for the plaintiff because the contract was clear and unambiguous.

You probably found the above exercises very simple. The point of these exercises was to make you aware of the different types of sentence patterns and to encourage you to use them in your writing. Those who are unaware of these things will usually produce dull and hard-to-follow prose.

Note: Many writing teachers recommend using short sentences for clarity. Some of them say that a sentence should generally be no more than 25 words. However, I think that the better approach is to listen to the sentences. If the clauses and phrases in the sentences flow together and adjoining sentences flow together, your sentence lengths are probably okay. In other words, I believe it is better to use judgment than mechanical rules.

Exercise 5-4

1. Look through a nonfiction book and identify the sentence patterns the author is using. Does the author use a variety of sentence patterns? Are his sentences choppy? Do the sentences flow together? How does the author's use of sentence patterns affect your opinion of the book? Could you have done a better job? Did the author use correct punctuation? Look at sentence patterns in other books.

2. Look through a document you have recently written. Do the sentences flow together smoothly, or do they seem choppy? Did you use a variety of sentence patterns? Did you use complex sentences? Did you use correct punctuation?

Pointers

1. Be aware of the different types of sentence patterns.
2. Use a variety of sentence patterns in your writing.
3. A series of short sentences is choppy. Combine short sentences for variety, coherence, and flow.
4. Learn the punctuation that goes with each type of sentence pattern.
5. Always think about the alternatives. Do not accept the first way of writing a sentence that pops into your mind.

Eliminate Redundant Sentences

Sometimes it is not necessary to combine sentences. A sentence may merely repeat what an earlier sentence said in different words. You should delete the redundant sentence.

> The children enjoyed the circus. They liked the clowns with their floppy ears and the animals, especially the horses and the elephants. The children had a lot of fun.
> The attorney objected to the letter's admissibility. There was no evidence that the victim had written it. Thus, it was not admissible.

In both cases, sentence three repeats the information contained in sentence one; the author should eliminate one of the sentences.

However, you should not eliminate sentences that add meaning. When sentences are partially redundant, eliminate the redundant parts or combine the sentences.

| **Pointer** |

Watch for redundant sentences and eliminate them. This is just like eliminating unnecessary words.

Don't Tread Water

Some sentences, while not redundant, tell the reader little. I call these sentences "empty sentences." Empty sentences slow down the development of your ideas, and they bore your readers. You should eliminate all sentences that tread water.

> California courts have decided many products liability cases. *Greenman* was the first California case to allow strict products liability. In *Greenman*, Justice Traynor held that a manufacturer who places a product on the market knowing that it is to be used without inspection is strictly liable when a defect in that product injures someone. Justice Traynor developed this rule because he felt that manufacturers, rather than consumers, should bear the costs of injuries from defective products. Manufacturers can buy insurance to provide for the possibility that someone will be injured by their products.

The first two sentences in the above paragraph convey little information to the reader; the writer should eliminate them. If the writer wants to let the reader know that *Greenman* was the first California case to allow strict products liability, he or she can do so in a supporting clause: "In *Greenman*, the first California case that allowed strict products liability, Justice Traynor . . ."

> An interesting case on this point is *Smith v. Jones*.
> This case is binding precedent in New York.
> By analyzing cases and statutes, one can make the following conclusions.

The above sentences also tread water.[1] Telling the reader that a case is interesting adds nothing to the reader's knowledge. Similarly, a lawyer will know that a case is binding precedent by looking at the citation. Likewise, lawyers usually make conclusions by analyzing cases and statutes; a writer wastes time by stating the obvious. Lawyers who use empty sentences are probably trying to pad their writing because they have little to say. You should expand your writing with details, not padding.

Exercise 5-5

Edit the following paragraph.

> *Walden v. Hernandez* is another case on personal jurisdiction. In this case, the court held that the defendant had established jurisdiction in California by signing the contract in California. Signing a contract in a state establishes minimum contacts with that state because the defendant is evoking the burdens and protections of a state's laws when she signs a contract in that state (*Kinkaid v. Schultz*). This principle is a basic one to personal jurisdiction law.

Answer
The first and fourth sentences tread water because they don't add anything to the discussion.

Pointers

1. Search your writing for empty sentences and eliminate them.
2. Expand your writing with details, not padding.

---

1. I have seen these sentences many times in my students' papers.

Paragraph Editing Exercises

Exercise 5-6

Edit the following paragraph employing the techniques you have learned from this book.

> Fran visited Europe last summer. Jan went with her. They spent three weeks in Europe. They first traveled to France. While in France, they visited Paris and Nice. Fran liked the Eiffel Tower. Jan liked the Louvre. Next, they went to Italy. They went to Venice, Florence, and Rome. They both liked the canals of Venice. They also liked the art of Florence. In Rome, they especially liked the churches. Jan and Fran ended their trip in Austria. They heard the Vienna Boys Choir. They also visited the palaces.

Answer

Fran and Jan spent three weeks in Europe last summer. They began their trip in France, where they visited Paris and Nice. Fran liked the Eiffel Tower; Jan liked the Louvre. Next, they went to Italy—Venice, Florence, and Rome. They enjoyed the canals of Venice, the art of Florence, and the churches of Rome. Fran and Jan ended their trip in Vienna, where they heard the Vienna Boys Choir and visited the palaces.

Exercise 5-7

Edit the following paragraph.

> John Wilson died yesterday in New York. He was 92 years old. John was born in Frankfort in the state of Kentucky. His parents were farmers. John attended the University of Kentucky. Later he went to law school at the University of Virginia. During World War II, he volunteered for service in the Navy. He fought in the Pacific. He received the Medal of Honor. After the war, he returned to Frankfort. He set

up a law practice. Beginning in 1952, he served four terms in the House of Representatives. In 1962, President Kennedy appointed John ambassador to West Germany. He spent six years as ambassador to West Germany. After he retired as ambassador in 1968, he joined the New York law firm of Wall & Street. He concentrated in the area of constitutional law. Random House published his memoirs in 1989.

Answer

John Wilson died in New York yesterday at the age of 92. John was born in Frankfort, Kentucky, where his parents were farmers. John attended the University of Kentucky and went to law school at the University of Virginia. During World War II, he volunteered for the Navy. He fought in the Pacific, and he received the Medal of Honor. After the war, he returned to Frankfort and set up a law practice. Beginning in 1952, he served four terms in the House of Representatives. In 1962, President Kennedy appointed John ambassador to West Germany. After he retired as ambassador in 1968, he joined the New York law firm Wall & Street, where he concentrated in constitutional law. Random House published his memoirs in 1989.

Exercise 5-8

Edit the following paragraph.

The defendant filed a counterclaim. The defendant claimed that the plaintiff had failed to negotiate a lease in good faith. This failure to negotiate caused the defendant to have to move shortly before the Christmas season. Thus, it lost a great deal of profits. The plaintiff made a good counterargument. The plaintiff countered that there is no good faith duty to negotiate a lease at common law. There isn't such a duty under statutory authority either. In addition, the plaintiff alleged that the failure to negotiate a new lease was the fault of the defendant. The defendant hadn't paid rent for four months. This was while negotiations were going on.

Answer

The defendant filed a counterclaim that alleged that the plaintiff had failed to negotiate a new lease in good faith. The defendant contended that this failure to negotiate in good faith caused it to lose significant profits because it had to move shortly before the Christmas season. The plaintiff countered that there is no good faith duty to negotiate a lease at common law or pursuant to statute. In addition, the plaintiff alleged that the failure to negotiate a new lease was the defendant's fault; it hadn't paid rent for four months during negotiations.

Exercise 5-9

Edit the following paragraph.

The witness testified that the traffic light was not functioning at the time of the accident. An attorney can object to testimony that is not allowed under the rules of evidence. The counsel of the plaintiff objected to the testimony of the witness. She did so because the witness had not seen the accident. The witness came to the intersection about two minutes after the accident. Thus, the witness could not testify that the light was not working at the time of the accident. The light could have been broken during the accident. The plaintiff's car ran into a telephone pole. The control box for the light was on the telephone pole. Thus, the testimony of the witness was not probative of the condition of the light at the time of the accident. The counsel of the plaintiff requested the court to exclude the testimony.

Answer

The witness testified that the traffic light was not functioning at the time of the accident. The plaintiff's counsel objected to this testimony because the witness had not seen the collision, having come to the intersection about two minutes after the accident. Thus, the witness could not testify that the light was not working at the time of the wreck. The light could have been broken when the plaintiff's car ran into the telephone pole that contained the light's control box.

Exercise 5-10

Edit the following paragraph.

Ludwig of Witten was the fifth king of Wittenstein. He ruled Wittenstein from 1856 to 1891. Many of his contemporaries considered him a great patron of the arts. Others believed that he only supported the arts for political reasons. During his reign, Wittenstein lost the prominence it had held in the region while his father was king. It also lost some of its area. Two hundred squares miles were ceded to Saxe-Witten. This occurred in 1885. This was pursuant to the Treaty of Prague. In his final years, Ludwig gave much of his power to his grandson. His grandson's name was Mark of Witten. Ludwig died in 1891. He was succeeded by a democratic government. This democratic government was headed by Mark of Witten.

Answer

Ludwig of Witten was the fifth king of Wittenstein, ruling from 1856 to 1891. Although many of his contemporaries considered him a great patron of the arts, others believed that he only supported the arts for political reasons. During his reign, Wittenstein lost the prominence it had held in the region while his father was king. It also ceded two hundred square miles to Saxe-Wittenberg in 1885 under the Treaty of Prague. In his final years, Ludwig gave much of his power to his grandson—Mark of Witten. After his death in 1891, Ludwig was succeeded by a democratic government, headed by Mark of Witten.

I hope you see that the answer is much better than the original in all the exercises. I also hope you understand why and that you can recognize these problems in your writing.

Do Not Overuse Particular Words within a Paragraph

Read the following paragraph:

Beck's Fifth Symphony is probably his most famous symphony. The symphony, written in 1885, is in four movements—Allegro, Largo, Minuet, and Rondo Finale. The symphony has an unusually large orchestra, including triple winds and organ in the symphony's last movement. Although the symphony was very popular before Beck's death, the symphony fell out of favor until Walter revived the symphony in 1968. Today, the symphony appears frequently on orchestra programs. The community orchestra will play the symphony next Sunday afternoon.

This paragraph is well written with one exception—the word "symphony" appears ten times. The overuse of symphony makes the paragraph sound stilted. You can improve the paragraph by deleting some appearances of symphony or by substituting other words.

Beck's Fifth Symphony is probably his most famous one. The work, written in 1885, is in four movements—Allegro, Largo, Minuet, and Rondo Finale. It has an unusually large orchestra, including triple winds and organ in the last movement. Although the symphony was very popular before Beck's death, it fell out of favor until Walter revived it in 1968. Today, the piece appears frequently on orchestra programs. The community orchestra will play the work next Sunday afternoon.

"Symphony" only appears twice in the revised version. I replaced it with synonyms (work, piece) and a pronoun (it), and I deleted it when it was unnecessary. Caveat: The overuse of synonyms can also make a passage sound stilted. You need to develop a careful balance between the extremes.

Exercise 5-11

Edit the following paragraph.

In 1979, the legislature passed a statute that regulates hazardous waste. The statute provides that all persons must dispose of hazardous waste in regulated facilities. Under the statute, the Environmental Board oversees such facilities. The statute provides severe penalties for violators, including criminal sanctions for certain acts forbidden by the statute. The statute also provides that out-of-state users may not use the facilities. The Supreme Court held this portion of the statute unconstitutional.

Answer

In 1979, the legislature passed a statute that regulates hazardous waste. This law requires that all persons must dispose of hazardous waste in regulated facilities, with the Environmental Board overseeing such sites. The statute provides severe penalties for violators, including criminal sanctions for certain acts. It also prohibits out-of-state users from employing the facilities. The Supreme Court held this portion unconstitutional.

Did you find two overused words in this example?

Exercise 5-12

Edit the following paragraph.

The defendant raises four arguments in support of defendant's motion to dismiss. Defendant first argues that subject matter jurisdiction is not proper in this court because the amount in controversy is under the statutory minimum. The defendant also argues that this court does not have jurisdiction over the defendant because the defendant lacks minimum contacts with this jurisdiction. The defendant then argues that this court is not the proper venue for this case because the defendant does not reside in this jurisdiction. Finally, the defendant argues that service of process was not proper because it was not made by certified mail.

Answer

The defendant presents four reasons to dismiss this action. He first argues that subject matter jurisdiction is not proper in this court because the amount in controversy is under the statutory minimum. He also contends that this court does not have personal jurisdiction over him because he lacks minimum contacts with this state. The defendant then asserts that this forum is not the proper venue for this case because he does not reside here. Finally, he states that service of process was not effective because it was not made by certified mail.

Pointer

Look through your paragraphs to make certain that you have not overused a particular word within that paragraph.

Avoid Abrupt Verb Tense Changes

A writer should not change the verb tense abruptly.[2] Often, a writer should use the same verb tense throughout a paragraph. However, the verb tense can change when the time switches. The following paragraph uses abrupt changes of verb tense.

John Doe published *A Theory of Law and Economics* in 1985. Doe believed that most bases of law are irrelevant. Rather, he theorizes that economics should be the basis of all law. He also thought that all law has an economic origin. For example, products liability law derived from an economic need to place the cost of injuries on the party most able to bear the cost—the manufacturer. Doe believes that even the

---

2. This is one of the biggest problems in my writing. I have to be especially attentive to abrupt changes of verb tense. If you have writing problems that keep reappearing in your writing, you should pay special attention to them when editing.

right of privacy has an economic basis. For example, the right to an abortion developed in the early 1970s simultaneously with women's increasing participation in the work force.

Do the abrupt verb changes in this example bother you? If they don't, you need to be more aware of the verb changes in your writing. Look at the corrected version next.

John Doe published *A Theory of Law and Economics* in 1985. Doe believed that most bases of law are irrelevant. Rather, he theorized that economics should be the basis of all law. He also thought that all law has an economic origin. For example, products liability law derived from an economic need to place the cost of injuries on the party most able to bear the cost—the manufacturer. Doe believed that even the right of privacy has an economic basis. For example, the right to an abortion developed in the early 1970s simultaneously with women's increasing participation in the work force.

Exercise 5-13

Fix the incorrect verb tenses in the following paragraph.

The majority ruled for the appellee, agreeing with the trial judge's decision that the will was not revoked by the decedent's remarriage. Judge Davis, writing for the majority, thinks that the legislature did not intend the statute to apply to a remarriage. On the other hand, Judge Martin in his dissent believed that the will was revoked, there being no exception to the statute. He presents several examples in his opinion where a remarriage might change the testator's intent.

Answer

The majority ruled for the appellee, agreeing with the trial judge's decision that the will was not revoked by the decedent's remarriage. Judge Davis, writing for the majority, thought that the legislature did not intend the statute to apply to a remarriage. On the other hand,

Judge Martin in his dissent believed that the will was revoked, there being no exception to the statute. He presented several examples in his opinion where a remarriage might change the testator's intent.

Pointer

Avoid abrupt changes of verb tense in your writing.

Exercise 5-14

Edit the following paragraph using the techniques found in this and earlier chapters.

> Copyright law is an important area of law. Copyright law has two theoretical bases. The first is based on an author's "natural rights." The second is based on a theory of economics. The theory of natural rights states that authors have a property right in their own work. This property right is just like a property right in a tangible thing, such as land. Thus, an author's copyright can only have the limitations that apply also to other kinds of property. On the other hand, the economic basis of copyright states that copyright is necessary to help encourage an author to create his works. Authors must receive an incentive, or they will not create. Thus, copyright should be limited to the protection needed to cause an author to create. Any greater rights would be wasteful. It would also deprive society of valuable rights that society could make efficient use of.

Answer

Copyright has two theoretical bases: (1) an author's "natural rights" and (2) economic theory. The natural rights theory states that authors have property rights in their works, which correspond to property rights in tangible things, such as land. Thus, a creator's copyright is limited only by the restrictions that apply to all property. On the other hand, economic theory claims that copyright is needed to encourage authors to create their works. Accordingly, Congress should limit copyright to the protection needed to fulfill this purpose. Any greater rights would be wasteful and would deprive society of valuable rights that it could use efficiently.

Conclusion

By now you should be reading your writing more carefully than you did before you started doing the exercises in this book. You should have also started to develop your inner ear for what sounds good and what doesn't. Finally, you should be more detail-oriented concerning your writing.

Chapter 6

Organizing Paragraphs and Creating Coherence

Chapter Goals

1. To make you aware of the importance of paragraph unity.
2. To show you how to make sure your paragraphs are unified.
3. To teach you how to start a paragraph with a striking topic sentence.
4. To make you aware of the importance of paragraph organization.
5. To help you understand how to organize a paragraph.
6. To show you how to put the sentences in a paragraph in logical order.
7. To introduce you to paragraph patterns.
8. To make you aware of the importance of coherence and flow within paragraphs.
9. To show you how to create coherence and flow within paragraphs.
10. To continue to help you carefully read and edit your writing.

Introduction

The structure of writing is hierarchical: Writing is organized on several levels—the phrase, sentence, paragraph, subsection, section, chapter, and so on. A good writer considers structure on all levels. Here are the typical levels of organization:

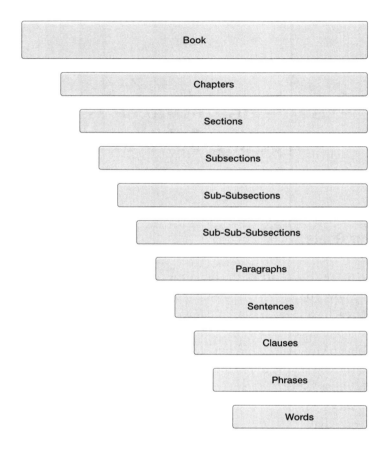

Previous chapters have concentrated on words, phrases, clauses, and sentences. I have shown you the various sentence patterns that exist in the English language, and how you can use particular patterns to create emphasis. This chapter will discuss three related topics: (1) paragraph unity, (2) paragraph organization, and (3) paragraph coherence and flow.

The paragraph is the basic unit of composition. Paragraphs indicate that you have switched to a new idea or subidea. A paragraph should not be too long; paragraphing helps readability. Similarly, paragraphs should not be too short. If a paragraph is too short, it means that you have not developed your ideas sufficiently. Although paragraphs generally contain four or five sentences, one should use a variety of paragraph lengths.

Pointers

1. Make sure that your paragraphs are not too long or too short.
2. Use a variety of paragraph lengths.

Paragraph Unity

Creating paragraph unity is an important part of writing paragraphs. First, paragraphs should contain only one subject or idea. Second, a paragraph should have a topic (thesis) sentence that introduces the subject of the paragraph. Third, all sentences in the paragraph should relate to the topic sentence.

While a paragraph may contain several ideas, it should include only one theme or main idea; there must be a justification for grouping sentences together. Each sentence in a paragraph should expand on the basic theme. If a part of the paragraph or a sentence sounds out of place, it probably is. You should delete it or move it.

The lower court found the defendant had unlawfully been carrying a concealed dirk or dagger in violation of Penal Code section 12020, subdivision (a) when he was stopped by a police officer. The issue is whether the knife-like instrument the minor had is a dirk or dagger within the meaning of that section. We conclude it is not and reverse . The instrument is a metal object three inches in length. The blade is one and a half inches long, curved on both sides, and beveled and sharpened on the front of one side. The flat side of the blade is smooth and approximately one-eighth inch thick, as is the remainder of the instrument. It has no handle and no guard to protect the hand from slipping onto the blade. It appears to be designed to fit between two fingers of the hand with the blade projecting outward. The top portion is smooth and slightly rounded to fit behind two fingers and into the palm of the hand.

I am sure that you recognized that the above paragraph was too long. In addition, it consists of two subjects: an introductory subject that summarizes the case and a description of the instrument. These are very different ideas. The writer should have started a new paragraph when she began discussing the knife.

Another aspect of paragraph unity is that every paragraph needs a clear topic sentence. A topic sentence presents the theme or idea of the paragraph. It is usually the first sentence of the paragraph, although occasionally it comes at the end. Do you see the problem in the following paragraph?

In *Smith*, the court said that "a seller generally does not have to disclose known defects when selling commercial real estate." *Kim* added that "a seller has to disclose known defects when selling commercial real estate when those defects involve serious safety or health concerns to human beings." However, *Williams* stated, "A seller does not have to disclose known defects when selling commercial real estate when those defects could be discovered through due diligence." Finally, *Rodriguez* declared, "A seller must disclose known economic liabilities and potential economic liabilities when selling commercial real estate."

The problem is that the paragraph lacks a clear topic sentence that sets out the paragraph's theme. The reader will probably not understand how the sentences relate to each other. An intelligent reader could probably eventually figure out the paragraph, but it is the writer's job to be clear. You cannot convince a reader that your ideas are legitimate if you put them in unclear prose. Here's a revision:

Although "a seller generally does not have to disclose known defects when selling commercial real estate," according to *Smith*, there are exceptions and exceptions to the exceptions. *Kim* declared that "a seller has to disclose known defects when selling commercial real estate when those defects involve serious safety or health concerns to human beings." However, *Williams* added, "A seller does not have to disclose known defects when selling commercial real estate when those defects could be discovered through due diligence." Finally, *Rodriquez* declared, "A seller must disclose known economic liabilities and potential economic liabilities when selling commercial real estate."

There is now a clear topic sentence in the revised example that tells the reader exactly what the paragraph is about. In this instance, the reader will understand the paragraph more quickly and is more likely to retain its idea. Here is another example of a paragraph that lacks unity:

John Jones was injured when a lathe he was working on malfunctioned. Jones's employer, KKE, bought the lathe six months ago from Lathes Are Us. Lathes Are Us gave no express warranties with the lathe, and it properly disclaimed all implied warranties. Jones lost two fingers in the accident and suffered severe cuts on his right arm. Jones incurred $10,000 in hospital bills from his injuries, and he is probably permanently disabled. After the malfunction, the lathe caught fire, damaging the lathe. Because the lathe is KKE's only lathe and because it cannot find a suitable replacement for the lathe, KKE will have to shut down for a month while the lathe is being repaired. Such a shutdown may cause KKE to file bankruptcy.

The above paragraph lacks unity because it encompasses too many unrelated ideas: (1) Jones's injury, (2) KKE's purchase of the lathe, (3) lack of warranties, (4) specification of Jones's injuries, (5) damage to the lathe, and (6) the fact that KKE will have to shut down while the lathe is being repaired. One can break the above paragraph into three paragraphs, each of which is unified.

John Jones, a KKE employee, was injured when a lathe he was working on malfunctioned. He lost two fingers in the accident and suffered severe cuts on his right arm. Jones incurred $10,000 in hospital bills from his injuries, and he is probably permanently disabled.

After the malfunction, the lathe caught fire, damaging the lathe. Because the lathe is KKE's only lathe and because it cannot find a suitable replacement for the lathe, KKE will have to shut down for a month while the lathe is being repaired. Such a shutdown may cause KKE to file bankruptcy.

KKE bought the lathe six months ago from Lathes Are Us. Lathes Are Us gave no express warranties with the lathe, and it properly disclaimed all implied warranties.

A paragraph should begin with a striking topic sentence. (The first sentence in a paragraph is the worst place for an empty sentence.) The topic sentence sets the paragraph's theme, and the remainder of the paragraph expands on the topic sentence. Each sentence in the paragraph should relate to the topic sentence.

Following World War I, Maurice Ravel developed a new attitude toward musical sound. Abandoning the sensuous harmonies that had previously characterized his music, he adopted harsh sonorities, which were the result of dense voicings of chords and liberal use of dissonance. In order to create new sound possibilities, he evolved a new harmonic vocabulary that added scales with conflicting inflections to the already established sources of scalar foundation. Most importantly, he constructed new kinds of texture in which simple layers were combined contrapuntally to form complex configurations or in which complex sonorities were sustained for long periods, creating the effect of stasis.

Note how the topic sentence sets out the theme of the paragraph: Ravel's new attitude toward sound. The remaining sentences give examples of the new types of sound Ravel used.

Exercise 6-1

Write at least five paragraphs with particular emphasis on producing a striking topic sentence.

Finally, all the sentences in the paragraph should relate to the topic sentence. If a sentence doesn't, delete it or put it somewhere where it is relevant. Can you see the problem in this paragraph?

Following World War I, Maurice Ravel developed a new attitude toward musical sound. Abandoning the sensuous harmonies that had previously characterized his music, he adopted harsh sonorities, which were the result of dense voicings of chords and liberal use of dissonance. In order to create new sound possibilities, he evolved a new harmonic vocabulary that added scales with conflicting inflections to the already established sources of scalar foundation. Most importantly, he constructed new kinds of texture in which simple layers were combined contrapuntally to form complex configurations or in which complex sonorities were sustained for long periods, creating the effect of stasis. Despite these changes, Ravel usually adopted traditional forms for his movements.

The last sentence doesn't fit with the other sentences. It concerns Ravel's use of form, while the other sentences involve his use of sound. Can you see the problem in the next paragraph?

The instrument is a metal object three inches in length. Donald was carrying it in his jacket pocket. The blade is one and a half inches long, curved on both sides, and beveled and sharpened on the front of one side. The flat side of the blade is smooth and approximately one-eighth inch thick, as is the remainder of the instrument. It has no handle and no guard to protect the hand from slipping onto the blade. It appears to be designed to fit between two fingers of the hand with the blade projecting outward. The top portion is smooth and slightly rounded to fit behind two fingers and into the palm of the hand.

All the sentences in the above paragraph concern the description of the instrument, except the second one, which tells the reader where Donald was carrying it. This may be an important idea, but it doesn't belong in this paragraph.

Exercise 6-2

Edit the following paragraphs for unity.

1. Following English common law, early American decisions did not recognize a wife's right to recover for loss of her husband's consortium. In 1950, the District of Columbia Circuit created an action for loss of a husband's consortium in order to achieve equality between the sexes. Since 1950, most courts have followed this holding, although a few jurisdictions have obtained equality by denying damages to both spouses. On the other hand, most courts have not extended compensation for loss of consortium to unmarried couples.

2. The defendant's conduct was intentional. Intentional means that the defendant intended to do the act. *Smith*. Intended does not require that the defendant intended the act's consequences. *Id*. Acme intended to call the plaintiff every hour for five days. The defendant's conduct caused the distress. To establish causation under this tort, the plaintiff must put on expert testimony that the defendant's conduct caused the plaintiff's emotional distress. *Id*. Dr. Robinson's testimony will help establish this element.

3. Finally, the plaintiff suffered severe emotional distress. The emotional distress necessary to establish intentional infliction of emotional harm must be more than is suffered in normal life. *Tate*. For example, having difficulty sleeping for a week is not severe emotional distress. *David*. This case also found that banging garbage cans outside the plaintiff's window every night for two weeks was outrageous. In this case, the defendant had to consult a psychologist to help her deal with the consequences of the harassment. She had trouble sleeping for several months, had vivid nightmares, and her hands often shook.

Answers

1. Following English common law, early American decisions did not recognize a wife's right to recover for loss of her husband's consortium. In 1950, the District of Columbia Circuit created an action for loss of a husband's consortium in order to achieve equality between the sexes. Since 1950, most courts have followed this holding, although a few jurisdictions have obtained equality by denying damages to both spouses. (The last sentence in the original does not go with the topic of the rest of the paragraph.)

2. The defendant's conduct was intentional. Intentional means that the defendant intended to do the act. *Smith*. Intended does not require that the defendant intended the act's consequences. *Id*. Acme intended to call the plaintiff every hour for five days.
   The defendant's conduct caused the distress. To establish causation under this tort, the plaintiff must put on expert testimony that the defendant's conduct caused the plaintiff's emotional distress. *Id*. Dr. Robinson's testimony will help establish this element. (This example should have been easy. There are two topics in the paragraph, so divide the paragraph into two.)

3. Finally, the plaintiff suffered severe emotional distress. The emotional distress to establish intentional infliction of emotional harm must be more than is suffered in normal life. *Tate*. For example, having difficulty sleeping for a week is not severe emotional distress. *David*. In this case, the defendant had to consult a psychologist to help her deal with the consequences of the harassment. She had trouble sleeping for several months, had vivid nightmares, and her hands often shook. (The sentence beginning "This case" is on a different topic. It may belong somewhere in the paper, but it does not belong in this paragraph.)

Pointers

1. Paragraphs should generally contain only one subject or idea. Always check your paragraphs to make sure that they are unified—that they have a clear topic sentence and that all sentences relate to the topic sentence.
2. Each paragraph should begin with a clear topic sentence.
3. Striking topic sentences grab your reader's attention.
4. All sentences in a paragraph should relate to the topic sentence.

Organizing Paragraphs

The sentences in a paragraph should be in a logical order. When a writer jumps around, the reader becomes confused. The writer should give the reader the information in the proper order. Consider the following examples:

> Should a child be compensated for loss of parental consortium? The correct position may be a compromise between two extremes: allowing compensation for certain elements of loss of consortium and denying it for others. Since 1980, at least seven jurisdictions have given such damages. However, during the same period, an equal number of states have refused to recognize this cause of action. Prior to 1980, no state had allowed recovery for loss of parental consortium. Previous articles on loss of parental consortium have either advocated complete recovery or none at all. This paper will discuss the emergence of compensation for loss of parental consortium and evaluate the wisdom of permitting such recovery.

Despite the fact that each sentence makes sense, the above paragraph is nonsense because the sentences aren't in a logical order. Look at the corrected version next:

> Should a child be compensated for loss of parental consortium? Prior to 1980, no state had allowed recovery for loss of parental consortium.

Since 1980, at least seven jurisdictions have given such damages. However, during the same period, an equal number of states have refused to recognize this cause of action. This paper will discuss the emergence of compensation for loss of parental consortium and evaluate the wisdom of permitting such recovery. Previous articles on loss of parental consortium have either advocated complete recovery or none at all. The correct position may be a compromise between these extremes: allowing compensation for certain elements of loss of consortium and denying it for others.

The problem in the next example is more subtle than in the above:

The plaintiff suffered severe emotional distress. For example, having difficulty sleeping for a week is not severe emotional distress. *David.* The emotional distress to establish intentional infliction of emotional harm must be more than is suffered in normal life. *Tate.* In this case, the defendant had to consult a psychologist to help her deal with the consequences of the harassment. She had trouble sleeping for several months, had vivid nightmares, and her hands often shook.

The problem in this paragraph is that I put the example before the principle. Here is a corrected version:

The plaintiff suffered severe emotional distress. The emotional distress to establish intentional infliction of emotional harm must be more than is suffered in normal life. *Tate.* For example, having difficulty sleeping for a week is not severe emotional distress. *David.* In this case, the defendant had to consult a psychologist to help her deal with the consequences of the harassment. She had trouble sleeping for several months, had vivid nightmares, and her hands often shook.

Let's look at another example with a different problem.

The plaintiff suffered severe emotional distress. In this case, the defendant had to consult a psychologist to help her deal with the consequences of the harassment. She had trouble sleeping for several months, had vivid nightmares, and her hands often shook. The emotional distress to establish intentional infliction of emotional harm must be more than is suffered in normal life. *Tate.* For example, having difficulty sleeping for a week is not severe emotional distress. *David.*

The problem in this paragraph is that I put the analysis before the principles the analysis is based upon. Lawyers will recognize that in writing a legal analysis, the writer should always put the law before the application. (For more on this topic, see Chapter 7.)

Exercise 6-3

Rearrange the sentences in a logical order.

1. Last night, Susan and I went to the opera, where we saw *Aida.* We plan to see *Faust* next week. We also sat around the Lincoln Center fountain before the curtain. The singers were excellent, and the orchestra played with passion. The performance was very good. We especially enjoyed the "Triumphal Scene." Before the opera, we had dinner at Clarke's.

2. Outrageous conduct is more than a person must endure in everyday life; minor insults, threats, or annoyances do not constitute outrageous conduct. *Smith.* The defendant's conduct was outrageous. A collection agency that uses normal means to collect a debt is not liable for intentional infliction of emotional harm. *Doe.* However, one court found that a collection agency sending a debtor over one hundred letters in six months was outrageous conduct. *Tate.* In fact, the conduct in this case is more severe than the bombardment of letters that *Tate* found to be outrageous because phone calls are more intrusive than letters and Acme called the plaintiff several times in the middle of the night. The defendant's conduct was not a normal means of collecting a debt; collection agencies do not call debtors every hour for five straight days.

Answers

1. Last night, Susan and I went to the opera, where we saw *Aida*. Before the opera, we had dinner at Clarke's. We also sat around the Lincoln Center fountain before the curtain. The performance was very good. The singers were excellent, and the orchestra played with passion. We especially enjoyed the "Triumphal Scene." We plan to see *Faust* next week.

2. The defendant's conduct was outrageous. Outrageous conduct is more than a person must endure in everyday life; minor insults, threats, or annoyances do not constitute outrageous conduct. *Smith*. A collection agency that uses normal means to collect a debt is not liable for intentional infliction of emotional harm. *Doe*. However, one court found that a collection agency sending a debtor over one hundred letters in six months was outrageous conduct. *Tate*.

   The defendant's conduct was not a normal means of collecting a debt; collection agencies do not call debtors every hour for five straight days. In fact, the conduct in this case is more severe than the bombardment of letters that *Tate* found to be outrageous because phone calls are more intrusive than letters and Acme called the plaintiff several times in the middle of the night.

Although all the sentences in the second answer are on the same topic, I divided them into two paragraphs for ease of reading.

There are numerous ways to organize paragraphs. Paragraph structure should generally derive from the content. However, there are several common paragraph patterns that a writer can employ.

The most common paragraph pattern comprises a topic sentence, followed by several sentences that expand on the theme, and a concluding sentence (topic, expansion, conclusion). A variation on this pattern consists of a topic sentence, followed by several sentences set off by numbers, then a concluding sentence.

This court does not have subject matter jurisdiction over this matter for three reasons. First, no federal question is involved. Second, the amount in controversy is less than the statutory minimum. Finally, both the plaintiff and defendant are citizens of North Carolina. Consequently, this court should grant the defendant's motion to dismiss.

In sum, the facts of this case demonstrate that the plaintiff should be able to recover for intentional infliction of emotional harm. First, the defendant's calling the plaintiff every hour for five days was outrageous. Second, the defendant made the calls. Third, expert testimony will establish that the defendant's conduct caused the harm. Finally, the plaintiff suffered severe emotional harm to the extent that she had to consult a psychologist.

Additional sentences can fill in the main ideas.

This court does not have subject matter jurisdiction over this matter. First, no federal question is involved. This suit concerns only state law tort issues. Second, the amount in controversy is less than the statutory minimum; at most, damages comprise $35,000. Finally, both the plaintiff and defendant are citizens of North Carolina. The plaintiff's domicile is Durham, and the defendant's principal place of business is Raleigh. Accordingly, this court should grant the defendant's motion to dismiss.

As is true of all paragraph patterns, one should not overuse the above pattern. It is particularly useful for introductions and conclusions.

Exercise 6-4

Write at least five paragraphs that use the above paragraph patterns. Make sure that the paragraphs are unified and that the sentences are in a logical order.

A paragraph can also have a deductive or inductive structure. A deductive structure starts with a general idea, then lists specifics. An inductive structure starts with the specific, then goes to the general.

Deductive: The Democratic Party is the party of the middle class. Democrats believe that the middle class is the bedrock of this country. Democrats support lower taxes for workers, higher taxes for corporations, and child-care credits. They also advocate greater funding for education and expanding the availability of student loans. Finally, they support a woman's right to an abortion.

Inductive: Republicans support traditional family values. They also believe in hard work and patriotism. Republicans oppose abortion, restrictions on school prayer, and pornography. They also favor limiting welfare and criminals' rights. Obviously, the Republican Party is the party of the middle class.

Similarly, a paragraph can start with the most important idea and go to the least important idea or start with the least important idea and build to the most important one.

Exercise 6-5

Write several paragraphs in two versions: the first with a deductive structure, the second with an inductive structure.

A writer can also organize paragraphs by using analogies. Analogies are particularly important in legal writing. In an analogy, the writer sets out one situation, then shows how it is analogous to another situation.

In *Bumpers v. Smith*, the court protected a bona fide purchaser for value, which is like protecting the holder in due course in this case. In *Bumpers*, the plaintiff gave her diamond necklace to a jeweler for repair. The jeweler then sold the necklace to the defendant at a fair price. When the plaintiff sued the defendant for return of the necklace, the court found for the defendant because he was a bona fide purchaser for value—he had no knowledge that the sale was wrongful and paid a fair price for the necklace. The case declared that the law favors bona fide purchasers for value. The same principle is the basis of the doctrine of holder in due course in negotiable instruments law. When a holder takes a check made out or endorsed to bearer for value and without notice of any defenses, she should be protected even though she took from a thief because she is a bona fide purchaser for value. The original owner could have protected himself by making the check out to order rather than bearer.

Exercise 6-6

Write several paragraphs using analogies.

A writer can also organize paragraphs chronologically. (A happened, then B happened, then C happened.) Chronological organization is especially useful for presenting a case's facts. Likewise, one can organize a paragraph spatially: imagine describing a museum as you walk through it. A paragraph can also be structured to build to a climax.

> Our tour visited the Louvre while we were in Paris. We first saw the Greek art, where we viewed the "Venus de Milo" and hundreds of vases. Next, our group moved to the ancient art, and we examined the "Code of Hammurabi." Our tour then proceeded to the painting collection to view the Mona Lisa. While in the painting section, we also saw French paintings by David and Delacroix. Finally, our group visited the Egyptian collection, and we left the museum by "Pei's Pyramid."

Exercise 6-7

Write several paragraphs using chronological, spatial, or climactic organization.

As was true of sentence patterns, good prose consists of a variety of paragraph organizations. Overuse of a particular paragraph structure can make your writing stiff. In addition, the type of paragraph organization depends on the content and the location in the paper or essay.

Exercise 6-8

Find an article in a magazine or an essay in a book and analyze the paragraph organization. Are the paragraphs well organized? Are the paragraphs unified? Do the paragraphs start with a clear topic sentence? Are the sentences in a logical order?

Pointers
1. Pay attention to paragraph organization.
2. Make sure the sentences in each paragraph are in a logical order.
3. Learn the different types of paragraph patterns.

Creating Coherence and Flow

Coherence and flow are important to effective writing. A paragraph may be technically perfect, but it will sound bad if the sentences do not flow together. This author believes that coherence and flow separate a good writer from a very good writer.

> This court should dismiss the plaintiff's complaint. This court lacks subject matter jurisdiction over the matter. No federal question is involved. This suit concerns only state law tort issues. The amount in controversy is less than the statutory minimum. The damages comprise at most $35,000. Both the plaintiff and defendant are citizens of North Carolina. The plaintiff's domicile is Durham. The defendant's principal place of business is Raleigh. This court should grant the defendant's motion to dismiss.

> This court does not have subject matter jurisdiction over this matter. First, no federal question is involved. This suit concerns only state law tort issues. Second, the amount in controversy is less than the

statutory minimum; at most, damages comprise \$35,000. Finally, both the plaintiff and defendant are citizens of North Carolina. The plaintiff's domicile is Durham, and the defendant's principal place of business is Raleigh. Accordingly, this court should grant the defendant's motion to dismiss.

Compare the two examples. In the second version, the sentences flow together. In addition, there is a sense of hierarchy; one can easily tell which ideas belong together and which are more important. In contrast, the first version sounds choppy, and there is no sense of hierarchy.

In the second version, the topic sentence sets up the organization. The structural use of "first," "second," and "third" creates a hierarchy (showing which ideas are more important and which ideas belong together) and produces coherence among the main ideas. "Accordingly"—a linking word—connects the body with the conclusion. Finally, in the rewritten version, some of the shorter sentences are combined.

There are many ways to create coherence and flow in a paragraph. The most important one is for the writer to think in large blocks—to think in units of several sentences instead of one sentence at a time. As I have stated in several contexts, it is very helpful to read your writing out loud. If your writing sounds choppy, it reads choppy.

Writing prose is much like composing music. A composer doesn't compose note by note or even phrase by phrase. Rather, a composer thinks in large blocks and establishes long-range goals. Music is constantly going forward toward a goal or relaxing from that goal. Each phrase has a dynamic curve; there are peaks and valleys of loudness and emphasis. For example, most musical phrases increase in loudness until about two-thirds of the way into the phrase, and then get softer. Phrases combine into larger groups, and these larger groups also possess a dynamic curve. The combination of phrases flows because of this dynamic curve and because one phrase derives from another. Finally, most works have a single goal (the climax) and a single large-scale dynamic curve.

Like music, prose has a dynamic curve. When you speak, your voice changes in tone and loudness depending on the emphasis desired, punctuation, and place in the sentence. When a writer is aware of the dynamics of the prose, he or she can use these dynamics to create continuity. Each sentence should have a dynamic curve, and the dynamic curves of adjacent sentences should flow together naturally. In addition, the writer should consider the dynamic flow of the paragraph. The curve should start with the topic sentence and push to the concluding one.

A composer also carefully organizes the phrases in order to create a coherent unit. Each phrase flows from the previous one. Phrases that belong together have only brief articulations between them, while medium-size units are separated by longer articulations. Repetitions connect phrases, and short transitional phrases connect longer units. Primary and subordinate material are properly placed.

In prose, each sentence should flow from the previous one. Phrases or sentences that belong together should use punctuation that produces brief pauses (commas, semicolons, etc.). Distinct units should be separated by long pauses (paragraph breaks). A writer can connect sentences by subtle repetitions and using connecting words or phrases (see below). The writer should properly place primary and subordinate materials.

Exercise 6-9

Recite Lincoln's Gettysburg Address. Note how your voice rises and falls in loudness and pitch. Examine the dynamic curve of each sentence, and how the dynamic curves of the sentences connect. Note the dynamic curve of the entire speech. Also examine how punctuation affects the pauses. If a recording is available, listen to it, and determine whether the reciter reads it the same way you do.

Do the same with Kennedy's inaugural address or another speech you admire. Listen to how the voice rises and falls in tone and pitch whenever you have the opportunity—when watching television, listening to lectures, and so on.

This section has presented general principles for making your writing flow. There are also mechanical means for creating coherence and flow. However, overuse of these devices will make your writing sound mechanical.

The most common mechanical device to create coherence is connecting (or transitional) words or phrases. Connecting words and phrases include moreover, furthermore, first, finally, in addition, on the other hand, to the contrary, in particular, for example, for instance, accordingly, consequently, therefore, shortly thereafter, thus, yet, however, next, similarly, likewise, also, in conclusion, obviously, today, thus far, and then. Consider the following examples.

1. We ate dinner at a French restaurant. Afterwards, we walked down Broadway and went to a movie. (afterwards)
2. The case does not support this argument. To the contrary, it demonstrates that copyright protection of compilations is limited. (to the contrary)
3. The above has demonstrated that this Court should dismiss this action. In particular, this Court lacks subject matter jurisdiction over this matter. (in particular)
4. *Smith* holds that jurisdiction must be based on the defendant's acts. Similarly, *Jones* holds that there is no personal jurisdiction unless the defendant has purposefully availed herself of acting in the jurisdiction. (similarly)
5. Harry failed the wills exam. Consequently, he will be attending summer school. (consequently)

Make sure you use the connecting word that conveys the connection between the sentences that you want.

1. We ate dinner at a French restaurant. Similarly, we walked down Broadway and went to a movie. (*Similarly* does not convey the proper connection between sentences.)
2. The case does not support this argument. In addition, it demonstrates that copyright protection of compilations is limited. (*In addition* does not indicate the proper relationship between the sentences.)

3. Harry failed the wills exam. Next, he will be attending summer school. (*Next* does not convey the best connection between the sentences.)

A writer can also create coherence by overlapping sentences—making a reference to a prior sentence at the beginning of the next sentence.

1. John spent five years in prison. While in prison, John learned how to read. (while in prison)
2. The witness testified concerning what she saw on November 15th. During her testimony, the witness identified John as the murderer. (during her testimony)
3. John stole some computer files from the company. When the company learned of the theft, it fired John and filed criminal charges against him. (when the company learned of the theft)

A writer can also use repetition of a key word to create coherence. However, one should be particularly careful not to overuse this technique.

1. Joy's favorite book is *Little People*. This book tells the story of the Smith family, who lived in England in the early 18th century. (book)
2. He had the experience to be president. This experience included twenty years in Congress and eight years as vice president. (experience)
3. She saw a light in the distance. The light came from the old lighthouse, although Joy did not know its source. (light)
4. Marge enjoyed Professor Johnson's class. Professor Johnson stressed the sociological basis of tort law and the lawyer's ethical duty. (Professor Johnson)
5. Leslie bought an IMM computer. Leslie's computer has two soft disc drives and a hard disc drive. (Leslie, computer)

Combining short sentences, as presented in Chapter 5, can also create coherence and flow. Again, the combined sentences should concern the same idea or flow from each other.

1. Margaret enjoys torts. She wants to be a personal injury lawyer. She also likes criminal law. She thinks it is exciting. (choppy)
2. Margaret enjoys torts. She wants to be a personal injury lawyer, and she also likes criminal law. She thinks it is exciting. (the wrong ideas are combined)
3. Margaret enjoys torts; she wants to be a personal injury lawyer. She also likes criminal law because she finds it exciting. (better)

Careful organization of paragraphs, as discussed above, also helps create coherence. In addition, unity of verb tense, mood, time, place, person, and so on can help unify a paragraph. Finally, a writer should use a variety of sentence lengths and patterns to avoid choppiness and establish flow and interest.

Exercise 6-10

Edit the following paragraph to create coherence.

> Joe's favorite sport is basketball. He likes the continuous action and frequent scoring. He likes tough inside play. He likes three-point shooting. His favorite team is the Bulls. They play in his hometown. His hometown is Chicago. They won the championship last year. They have his favorite player, Michael Jordan. He also likes John Paxson. Joe went to 20 home games last year. He watched the rest of the games on television.

Answer

> Joe's favorite sport is basketball because of the continuous action and frequent scoring. He also likes tough inside play and three-point shooting. Joe's favorite basketball team is his hometown Chicago Bulls, who won the championship last year. The Bulls have Joe's favorite players, Michael Jordan and John Paxson. Joe went to 20 Bulls games last year, and he watched the rest on television.

I created coherence in the above paragraph by combining sentences and employing subtle repetitions. I also used a connecting word (also).

Exercise 6-11

Edit the following paragraph to create coherence.

> Copyright is an intangible property right. It is an intellectual property right. It protects an author's rights in writings. Writings include paintings, sculpture, and music. Copyright attaches when a work is "fixed." Fixed means fixed in a tangible medium. Registration is not required for a valid copyright. Registration does allow recovery of "statutory" damages. It allows recovery of attorney's fees. Notice is not required for copyright protection. This has changed since adoption of the Berne Convention.

Answer

> Copyright is an intangible, intellectual property right. It protects an author's rights in writings, which include paintings, sculpture, and music. Copyright attaches when a work is "fixed" in a tangible medium. Registration is not required for a valid copyright. However, registration allows recovery of "statutory" damages and attorney's fees. Like registration, notice is not required for copyright protection since adoption of the Berne Convention.

Exercise 6-12

Edit the following paragraph.

> Our class visited Mammoth Cave last Saturday. It is the longest cave in the world. It is over 300 miles long. We took a two-hour tour of the cave. We entered the cave through a natural entrance. We came upon a large room. This room is called the "Rotunda." We went through a wide cave passage. We descended to a lower level of the cave. We

passed a large pit. The pit is called "Bottomless Pit." We went through "Fat Man's Misery." We ascended through "Mammoth Dome." We came upon the "Rotunda" again. We left the cave by the natural entrance.

Answer

Last Saturday, our class visited Mammoth Cave—the longest cave in the world (over 300 miles long). We took a two-hour tour of the cave. Our tour entered the cave through a natural entrance, and soon we came upon a large room called the "Rotunda." We then traveled through a wide cave passage. Next, our tour descended to a lower level of the cave, passing a large pit named "Bottomless Pit." We then crowded through "Fat Man's Misery," and we ascended through "Mammoth Dome." After our tour reached the "Rotunda" again, we left the cave by the natural entrance.

Pointers

1. To create coherence and flow, think in large blocks (an entire paragraph).
2. To create coherence and flow, read your writing out loud and listen carefully.
3. Listen for the dynamic curves in your writing.
4. Listen to how the sentences fit together.
5. Listen for the flow that connects sentences.
6. Carefully organize the phrases to create a coherent unit.
7. Use punctuation to create flow and coherence. (Short and long pauses produced by punctuation.)
8. Use transitional words and phrases to connect sentences.
9. Repeat words to create connections between sentences.
10. Combine sentences to create coherence and flow.
11. Carefully organize paragraphs to create coherence and flow.
12. Use a variety of sentence patterns to help create coherence and flow.
13. Paragraph unity helps create coherence and flow.

Conclusion

In addition to learning the details of writing paragraphs, you should now be reading your writing more closely and carefully. Often, fixing a problem is easy once you have found it. The hard part is recognizing the problems in your writing.

Chapter 7

The Small-Scale Paradigm

Chapter Goals

I started the last chapter with a chart of the levels of organization of a book. Among these levels were sections, subsections, sub-subsections, and sub-sub-subsections. Lawyers usually organize these parts in the argument sections of briefs to the court or the discussion section of an objective memorandum using a small-scale paradigm. This chapter will present a small-scale paradigm that you can use in these parts.

Small-Scale Paradigm Defined

A small-scale paradigm is the basic unit of organization of a legal analysis or argument. It is how one organizes a single issue with no subissues or how one organizes a subissue or sub-subissue.[1] In other words, an argument or discussion section will usually contain several small-scale paradigms.

The basic structure of a small-scale paradigm is based on how a writer should organize a simple legal analysis or argument: **issue, law, analysis** (application of the law to the facts), and **conclusion**. This organization is necessary because the reader needs to know what the law is before he or she can understand how the law applies to the facts of the case. In other

---

1. I will demonstrate how the small-scale paradigm fits within medium- and large-scale organization in the next chapter.

words, this is the most logical way to present a legal argument or analysis. This general structure is the basis of the small-scale paradigm you learned in law school, such as IRAC (issue, rule, analysis, conclusion).

I have based my small-scale paradigm on the above general structure. It mainly differs from other small-scale paradigms in that it goes into more detail and begins with the conclusion. My small-scale paradigm is as follows:[2]

Small-Scale Paradigm Outline

Conclusion
Law: Rule
    Rule Explanation
    Rule Illustration(s)
Application: Apply the Principles (Rule Application)
    Case Comparison(s)

Conclusion

The paradigm begins with a one-sentence conclusion for clarity. I have put the conclusion first because it is easier for a reader to understand the analysis when he knows what the conclusion is. (The issue, of course, is part of the conclusion in my paradigm.) For example, a conclusion might be, "The 1954 Act is unconstitutional under the Establishment Clause because the act's purpose was to advance religion."

---

2. I have synthesized this paradigm from a number of sources, including Richard K. Neumann, Jr., *Legal Reasoning and Legal Writing: Structure, Strategy, and Style*, 97–143 (Aspen Pub., 5th ed. 2005); Helene S. Shapo, Marilyn R. Walter, & Elizabeth Fajans, *Writing and Analysis in the Law*, 113–29 (Foundation Press, Rev. 4th ed. 2003); and Linda Edwards, *Legal Writing and Analysis*, 89–108 (Little, Brown and Co., 2003). I have given the details of the theoretical basis of this paradigm in E. Scott Fruehwald, *Think Like a Lawyer: Legal Reasoning for Lawyers and Business Professionals*, 164–65 (ABA Pub., 2013). You do not need to understand the theoretical basis of the small-scale paradigm to use it.

Law

Rule

The law section should begin with a clear statement of the rule (usually one sentence). This is important for clarity because it tells the reader at the beginning of the law section what the rule is. The rest of the law section will then explain and illustrate the rule.

You must synthesize the rule from all the relevant cases and other legal material, unless a case has already done the synthesis.[3] Even if a case has already done the synthesis, you must ascertain that later cases have not changed the rule. (Example of a rule: "To be constitutional under the Establishment Clause, a statute must have a secular purpose.")

Rule Explanation

The rule explanation explains the rule, expands on the rule, and gives the policy behind the rule. It usually proceeds from the general to the specific, going from a general explanation of the rule to a specific explanation of the law as it applies to the facts of your case. This is a very important section because the meaning of the rule will usually not be clear from just the statement of the rule. For example, assume the rule for this subsection is "To be constitutional under the Establishment Clause, a statute must have a secular purpose." What does *secular purpose* mean? You should help the reader understand the rule by taking material from a variety of cases, making the rule explanation a synthesis of the law. The rule explanation is also important because it usually includes discussion of the policy behind the rule. Here's an example of conclusion, rule, and rule explanation:

> The 1954 Act, which altered the Pledge of Allegiance to include the words "under God," violates the Establishment Clause because it does not have a secular purpose. [←conclusion] [rule→] The purpose prong of the endorsement test requires that a statute have a secular purpose. *Lynch*, 465 U.S. at 680 (O'Connor, J. concurring). [←rule] [rule explanation→] This requirement is not satisfied by the mere existence of

---

3. I discuss how to synthesize a rule in Fruehwald, *Think Like a Lawyer*, at 99–119. It is not necessary for you to read this chapter to understand how my small-scale paradigm works. However, it will be useful to you if you have problems synthesizing rules from cases.

some secular purpose as the purpose must be wholly secular. *Id.* at 700 (O'Connor, J. concurring). It is a violation of the Establishment Clause whenever the government intends to convey a message of endorsement or disapproval of religion through a statute. *Id.* (O'Connor, J. concurring). Government cannot pass laws that aid religion, as the Establishment Clause creates a wall to separate church and state and that wall must be kept high and impregnable. *Everson v. Bd. of Educ.*, 330 U.S. 504, 512 (1947). This wall is the main reason the Establishment Clause was enacted—to prevent a governmental decision maker from abandoning neutrality and acting with the intent of promoting a particular point of view in religious matters. *Wallace v. Jaffree*, 472 U.S. 38, 59 (1985). [←rule explanation]

Rule Illustration

A rule illustration uses one or more cases to show how the rule works in a factual context (an example), and it helps set up the case comparison(s) in the application. The case or cases for the rule illustration should usually be as close as possible to the facts of the main case. In the first sentence of the rule illustration, you should tell the reader why the case is being cited. In other words, you should start with the holding, focusing on the topic of the section or subsection. Then, you should give the facts and reasoning of the case, again focusing on the topic of the section or the subsection. You should leave out anything that is irrelevant. Whether you use one rule illustration or two or three depends on the complexity of the issue or subissue and how good the cases are. However, having at least two rule illustrations allows for both reasoning by analogy and distinguishing cases.

Rule Illustration Outline
> Topic sentence (holding)
> Facts of the case
> Reasoning of the case

Here's an example of rule illustration:

In *Montez*, the court held that there was a cause of action for loss of spousal consortium. [←topic sentence: holding] [→facts] In this case, Mr. Montez had been badly injured in a traffic accident that was the defendant's fault. After the accident, Mr. Montez was confined to a wheel chair, and he was unable to have sexual relations with his wife. [←facts] [→reasoning] The court reasoned that Mrs. Montez should be able to recover for loss of consortium because she had suffered a cognizable injury. Her husband was not able to provide her the companionship he had previously, and he was no longer able to have sexual relations with her. [←reasoning]

Application
Apply the Principles
After having fully presented the law, you should apply the law to the facts *in detail*. In other words, you should show how the facts fit into the above law. You should start by applying the principles and save the case comparisons for last. The purpose of case comparisons is to strengthen the analysis, not substitute for the analysis. Here's an example of application of law to facts:

Mary's website is transformative because it adds something new to the original since it includes her drawings of the show, discussions of the characters, a discussion of the show's themes, and biographies of the show's stars, all of which alter the original with new expression and meaning. It also has a different purpose than the original. *Bold*'s purpose is entertainment, while Mary's website is informative. The website does not supersede the original; rather, it helps explain the show. Because it adds to the original, the website satisfies copyright's purpose in advancing the arts and the sciences.

Case Comparison
The case comparison should begin with a topic sentence that summarizes the comparison. You then should give a detailed comparison of the facts of the two cases (the rule illustration and your case), showing how they are similar. There is no need to show similarities between the cases that are not

material to the comparison.[4] Next, you should include any reasoning from the cases to back up the factual comparison. Finally, you should end with a conclusion that demonstrates why the comparison is important to your case.

Case Comparison Outline
    Topic sentence that presents the comparison
    Comparison of facts
    Comparison of reasoning
    Conclusion and relation to case

Here's an example of case comparison:

> This court should allow the Jenkins children to recover for the loss of their father's consortium, just like the court allowed recovery for loss of spousal consortium in *Montez*. [←topic sentence that presents the comparison] [comparison of facts→] While, in this case, there was no loss of sexual relations, as there was in *Montez*, the justification for recovery is even stronger here than it was in *Montez*. Mr. Jenkins's injuries were much more severe than Mr. Montez's. While Mr. Montez was confined to a wheelchair, he was still able to use his arms and converse with his wife. Here, Mr. Jenkins is a quadriplegic, and he suffered a brain injury that prevents him from talking. [←comparison of facts] [comparison of reasoning→] The reasoning from *Montez* applies here, too. The Jenkins children have suffered a cognizable injury because they have lost the companionship of their father, who was the most important person in their lives. [←comparison of reasoning] [conclusion→] Therefore, this court should allow Joey and Lisa Jenkins to recover for loss of parental consortium.

Instead of showing the similarities between the rule illustration and your case in the case comparison, you can show the differences in order to

---

4. The comparison is not of the whole of the precedent case with your case. It is the differences between the comparison case and your case on a particular issue or subissue. That the cases can be distinguished on a separate issue or subissue is irrelevant.

distinguish your case. Here's an example of case comparison that distinguishes the rule illustration:

[First rule illustration omitted.]

[second rule illustration➔] In contrast, in *American Geophysical*, 510 U.S. at 913, the court held that photocopying articles for laboratory use was not transformative. In this case, Texaco had photocopied magazine articles from journals it had subscribed to, so they would be in a more usable format for the laboratory. The court noted that when, as in this case, the secondary use is merely an untransformed duplication, the value generated by this use is little more than the value of the original. *Id.* at 923. Thus, "Texaco's photocopying merely transforms the material object embodying the intangible article that is the copyrighted original work." *Id.*

[Application of law to facts omitted.]

[First case comparison omitted.]

[second case comparison➔] In contrast, Mary's website is not like the copying in *American Geophysical* because it is much more than the photocopying in that case. Unlike *American Geophysical*, in which the use was merely untransformed copying, Mary's website adds value to the original with its original material. Because of the original material, it does much more than embody the original intangible article that was found not to be transformative in *American Geophysical*.

Here is an example of a complete small-scale paradigm:[5]

I. CONGRESS'S 1954 AMENDMENT TO THE PLEDGE OF ALLEGIANCE IS UNCONSTITUTIONAL UNDER THE ESTABLISHMENT CLAUSE BECAUSE IT FAILS THE ENDORSEMENT TEST, SINCE IT SENDS A MESSAGE TO ATHEISTS AND BELIEVERS OF NON-MONOTHEISTIC RELIGIONS THAT

---

5. []= first-level divisions; ()=second-level divisions (divisions within the first level); {}=third-level divisions (divisions within the second level).

MONOTHEISM IS PREFERRED BASED ON THE BELIEF IN THE EXISTENCE OF ONE GOD.

The 1954 Amendment to the Pledge of Allegiance is unconstitutional under the "endorsement test" because the words "under God" convey a message that the government prefers monotheism, making non-adherents feel like outsiders. [◀conclusion] [law➡] (rule➡) Government endorsement of a religion or disapproval of a religion is unconstitutional. *County of Allegheny*, 492 U.S. at 593–594; *see also Lynch*, 465 U.S. at 689 (O'Connor, J., concurring). (◀rule) (rule explanation➡) Endorsement of religion "sends a message to non-adherents that they are outsiders and not full members of the political community, and an accompanying message to adherents that they are insiders, favored members of the political community." *Lynch*, 465 U.S. at 688 (O'Connor, J., concurring). The endorsement test focuses on the character of the government activity and any message that might cause divisiveness. *Id.* It does not stop Congress from considering religion when passing statutes, but it does "preclude [it] from conveying or attempting to convey a message that religion or a particular religious belief is favored or preferred." *Wallace*, 472 U.S. at 70. Congress cannot pass laws that aid religions "based on a belief in the existence of God as against those religions founded on different beliefs." *Wallace*, 472 U.S. at 55. (◀rule explanation)

(rule illustration➡) In *County of Allegheny*, the Court held that a creche on public property conveyed an endorsement of the Christian praise to God, while a menorah beside a Christmas tree did not impart a governmental endorsement of Judaism. *Id.* at 598, 614. {◀topic sentence—holding}{facts of the case➡} The creche was located by itself in the most beautiful area of the courthouse, while the menorah was placed next to a Christmas tree. {◀facts of the case} {reasoning of the case➡} The Court found that the creche's highly religious nature combined with its physical location by itself in the most beautiful area of a courthouse would send the message that it was placed there with "the support and approval of the government." *Id.* at 599–600. In contrast, an observer would not "sufficiently likely" interpret the menorah, a religious symbol of Judaism, as an endorsement of religion but as a secular recognition of tradition because it was located beside a Christmas tree. *Id.* at 620. The Court reasoned that when a government's message is conveyed by a religious symbol and that message could be conveyed by either a religious or secular symbol, it may lead an observer to infer that the government is trying to endorse a particular religious faith. *Id.* at 618. The Court felt that the creche had the secular alternative of a Christmas tree, but the menorah had no secular alternative. Consequently, the Court held that the creche was unconstitutional because it sent a message to non-adherents that they were outsiders and not full members of the political community. *Id.* at 598. {←reasoning of the case} (←rule illustration) [application→] (applying the principles→) The 1954 Amendment conveys a message that the United States government is endorsing monotheism at the expense of atheism and non-monotheistic religions. The purpose of the addition to the Pledge is wholly religious. The words "under God" not only appear in the Pledge symbolizing commitment to American values, they appear in a context of significant importance: The Pledge reads "one nation, under God, indivisible." This context sends a message that the United States is guided by, and solidified by, a common bond and belief in one Supreme Being. This conveys a message to atheists and non-monotheistic believers that they are not part of the solidified country and do not agree with the belief in one Supreme Being, which is basic to this country's values. The 1954 Amendment aids religions based on the belief in God by spreading a message that God exists and is a part of the United States, which makes non-adherents feel like outsiders when they are forced to recite the pledge or simply hear it being recited. The appellee's daughter testified that she felt "embarrassed and stupid" when other students stood and said the pledge, which demonstrates how "under God" sends a message to nonbelievers that they are outsiders. (←applying the principles)

(case comparison→) This case is similar to *Allegheny* in that, while the United States may have been trying to express a secular message, instead of using a secular symbol, Congress chose to use the words "under God" to send its message. {←topic sentence that presents the comparison}{comparison of facts➜} Like the creche in *Allegheny* and unlike the menorah in that case, the words "under God" stand alone, without any secular symbol to negate their impact. {⬅comparison of facts} {comparison of reasoning➜} Because of this, a hearer of the Pledge will "sufficiently likely" interpret the words as an endorsement of religion, like the Court interpreted the creche by itself as endorsing religion in *Allegheny*. In both cases, a government's message is conveyed by a religious symbol and that message could be conveyed by either a religious or secular symbol. {conclusion and relation to case➜} Since the Pledge contains the words "under God," the 1954 Amendment forces non-adherents to feel like outsiders, just as the creche did in *Allegheny*, and the 1954 Amendment is unconstitutional. {⬅conclusion and relation to case}(⬅case comparison) [⬅application]

The small-scale paradigm can be any length. The length will be dictated by the complexity of the issue, the law, and the facts of your case. Similarly, it can consist of any paragraph construction, again depending on the complexity of the material. The following gives you two examples of how you might paragraph a small-scale paradigm.

Small-Scale Paradigm and Paragraphing Outline

Example: Short Paradigm
Paragraph I:
   Conclusion
   Rule
   Rule Explanation
Paragraph II:
   Rule Illustration
Paragraph III:
   Application of Law to Facts
   Case Comparison

More Complex Paradigm Outline

Paragraph I:
  Conclusion
  Rule
  Rule Explanation
Paragraph II:
  First Rule Illustration
Paragraph III:
  Second Rule Illustration
Paragraph IV:
  Application of Law to Facts
Paragraph V:
  First Case Comparison
Paragraph VI:
  Second Case Comparison

The following are common problems in the small-scale paradigm:

1. The conclusion is not clearly stated at the beginning. It is clearer if the writer starts the analysis with the conclusion, rather than the issue or the law.

2. The writer starts to apply the facts before discussing the law. After the one-sentence conclusion, you should start the rule section. Otherwise, you will confuse your reader.

3. The rule section does not begin with a clear rule. An analysis is easier to understand if you start the law with the rule then explain what the rule means.

4. The rule explanation is too general. Part of the rule explanation should explain how the rule specifically applies to the facts. Tailor the law to your case, and be careful how you choose cases.

5. The writer has not fully explained the rule.

6. The rule explanation does not synthesize the reasoning from the relevant cases.

7. The sentences in the rule explanation are not in a logical order. You usually go from the general to the specific in the rule explanation.

8. The rule or a sentence in the rule explanation starts with a case name. In the rule and rule explanation, emphasize the principle, not the case. For example, don't start a sentence "In *Burger King* . . ."; rather, put the cite at the end of the sentence.

9. The cases used in the rule illustration are not close to the facts in your case. Spending time on research pays off!

10. The rule illustrations include irrelevant material (not on issue).

11. The rule illustration does not start with the case holding.

12. The rule illustrations don't add to the reader's understanding of the law. It is often helpful to have two rule illustrations. However, do not add a rule illustration just to take up space.

13. The case holding does not emphasize the topic of the section.

14. The rule illustration does not follow the model given above (holding-facts-reasoning).

15. The law is not fully explained through the rule explanation and rule illustrations. Your reader should not have to look outside your paper to understand the law. It is the writer's responsibility to educate the reader in the law.

16. The rule application does not apply the law from the rule and rule explanation. Apply the law to the facts in detail.

17. The case comparison(s) does not follow the model given above (sentence that presents the comparison-comparison of facts-comparison of reasoning-conclusion and relation to case).

18. The case comparisons are not in detail.

19. The case comparisons include matter that is not relevant to the issue.

20. Two rule illustrations are given, but case comparisons for both are not given.

21. The paradigm is not easily readable on the first reading. It is the author's duty to be as clear as possible.

Labeling the parts in your small-scale paradigms, as I have done in my examples, can help you see the problems in your small-scale paradigms.[6]

---

6. Of course, you should take them out before you file the brief with the court or let another attorney see it.

Exercises

Finding Problems in the Small-Scale Paradigm

1. Identify the problem with the following small-scale paradigm. (It stops before the application.)

Mary's website is transformative of the show *Bold* because it presents the show's material in a new form. A use is transformative if it adds something new to the original with a further purpose or different character, altering the original with new expression, meaning, or message. *Campbell v. Acuff-Rose*, 510 U.S. 569, 579 (1994); see also *Blanch v. Koons*, 467 F.3d 244, 251-52 (2d Cir. 2006) (Does the secondary use add value to the original?); *American Geophysical Union v. Texaco, Inc.*, 60 F.3d 913, 923 (2d Cir. 1994) ("The 'transformative use' concept is pertinent to a court's investigation under the first factor because it assesses the value generated by the secondary use and the means by which such value is generated"). In *Warner Bros. Entertainment, Inc. v. RDR Books*, 575 F. Supp. 2d 513 (S.D.N.Y. 2008), a court held a Harry Potter Lexicon book to be transformative because it served as a reference work. The author's purpose in writing the book was "to create an encyclopedia that collected and organized information from the Harry Potter books in one central source for fans to use for reference." *Id*. In analyzing the lexicon, the court stated, "Presumably, Rowling created the Harry Potter series for the expressive purpose of telling an entertaining and thought-provoking story centered on the character Harry Potter and set in a magical world. The Lexicon, on the other hand, uses material from the series for the practical purpose of making information about the intricate world of Harry Potter readily accessible to readers in a reference guide." *Id*. The court concluded, "Because it serves these reference purposes, rather than the entertainment or aesthetic purposes of the original works, the Lexicon's use is transformative and does not supplant the objects of the Harry Potter works." *Id*.

In contrast, in *American Geophysical*, 510 U.S. at 913, the court held that photocopying articles for laboratory use was not transformative.

In this case, Texaco had photocopied magazine articles from journals it had subscribed to, so they would be in a more usable format for the laboratory. The court noted that when, as in this case, the secondary use is merely an untransformed duplication, the value generated by this use is little more than the value of the original. *Id.* at 923. Thus, "Texaco's photocopying merely transforms the material object embodying the intangible article that is the copyrighted original work." *Id.*

2. Identify the problem in the following small-scale paradigm. (It is the application section of the paradigm.)

Mary's website is transformative. Like the Harry Potter Lexicon, its purpose is to make information about the show available to the public. It contains Mary's drawings, her discussion of the characters, her discussion of the show's themes, and her biographies of the actors, similar to the material in the lexicon. Also like the lexicon, the website lacks the entertainment or aesthetic value of the original. Consequently, Mary's website is transformative, just like the Harry Potter Lexicon. In contrast, Mary's website is not like the copying in *American Geophysical* because it is much more than the photocopying in that case. Unlike *American Geophysical*, in which the use was merely untransformed copying, Mary's website adds value to the original with its original material. Because of the original material, it does much more than embodying the original intangible article that was found not to be transformative in *American Geophysical*.

3. Identify the problems with the small-scale paradigm in the following paragraph. (It is the first paragraph of a small-scale paradigm.)

The first issue is whether Mary's website is transformative of the show *Bold*. A use is transformative if adds something new to the original with a further purpose or different character, altering the original with new expression, meaning, or message. *Campbell v. Acuff-Rose*, 510 U.S. 569, 579 (1994); see also *Blanch v. Koons*, 467 F.3d 244, 251–52

(2d Cir. 2006) (does the secondary use add value to the original?); *American Geophysical Union v. Texaco, Inc.*, 60 F.3d 913, 923 (2d Cir. 1994) ("The 'transformative use' concept is pertinent to a court's investigation under the first factor because it assesses the value generated by the secondary use and the means by which such value is generated"). On the other hand, an untransformed use usually has the same intrinsic purpose as the original, limiting any justification for fair use. *American Geophysical*, 510 U.S. at 923. The new work should not merely supersede the objects of the original. *Campbell*, 510 U.S. at 579. Transformative works lie at "the heart of the fair use doctrine's guarantee of breathing space within the confines of copyright" because they further the goal of copyright—to promote science and the arts. *Id.*

4. Identify the problems in this rule illustration.

   In *Wallace v. Jaffree*, a statute authorized a daily period of silence in public schools for voluntary prayer. The school would designate a specific time of each day for students to either meditate or pray for their respective religion. The court reasoned this statute to violate the establishment clause because the purpose was to advance religion by returning prayer to public schools. *Id.* Because the purpose was wholly religious and nonsecular, the court declared this statute unconstitutional and a direct violation of the Establishment Clause. *Id.*

5. Identify the problem in this application section.

   Mary's website is transformative because it adds something new to the original. Like the lexicon in *Warner Bros*, Mary's website serves as a reference work. Like the Harry Potter Lexicon, its purpose is to make information about the show available to the public. It contains Mary's drawings, her discussion of the characters, her discussion of the show's themes, and her biographies of the actors, similar to the material in the lexicon. Also like the lexicon, the website lacks the entertainment or aesthetic value of the original. Consequently, Mary's website is transformative, just like the Harry Potter Lexicon.

6. Identify the problems in this application of the law to the facts. (It stops before the case comparison.)

In the present case, Sarah's teacher, Ms. Kennedy, led the class in recitation of the Pledge, with the words "under God" as a daily routine. The United States government added the words "under God" in a 1954 Act with the purpose of advancing religion. As the legislative history of the 1954 Act sets forth: "The human person is important because he was created by God . . . The inclusion of God in our Pledge therefore would further acknowledge the dependence of our people and our government upon the moral directions of the Creator . . . At the same time it would serve to deny atheistic concepts." (R. 3.) The purpose of the amendment is clearly nonsecular as it is taking a strong position on the question of theism, namely to support the existence and moral authority of God, while denying atheistic ideals. Such a purpose runs counter to the Establishment Clause, which prohibits the government endorsement of religion. Because the1954 Act clearly does not have a secular purpose, it plainly violates the Establishment Clause.

7. Critique this case comparison.

Wallace and this case are extremely similar with regard to whether the government conduct in question, a statute regarding religion, has a secular purpose. Both involve statutes that were enacted to advance religion, with wholly nonsecular purposes. In *Wallace*, the purpose of the statute was to bring prayer back to public school with the intent of advancing religion, similar to the current case where the purpose of the act was to support the existence of God, also advancing religion. Because of the extreme similarity in facts with regard to the first prong of the endorsement test, this should lead to a similar ruling. The court ruled in *Wallace* that the statute was in violation of the

Establishment Clause because the purpose was nonsecular, and that should be the case here.

8. Critique this paradigm. (It stops before the rule illustration.)

The 1954 Amendment to the Pledge of Allegiance is unconstitutional under the "endorsement test" because the words "under God" convey a message that the government prefers monotheism, making non-adherents feel like outsiders. Endorsement of religion "sends a message to non-adherents that they are outsiders and not full members of the political community, and an accompanying message to adherents that they are insiders, favored members of the political community." *Lynch*, 465 U.S. at 688 (O'Connor, J., concurring). The endorsement test focuses on the character of the government activity and any message that might cause divisiveness. *Lynch*, 465 U.S. at 689 (O'Connor, J., concurring). It does not stop Congress from considering religion when passing statutes, but it does "preclude [it] from conveying or attempting to convey a message that religion or a particular religious belief is favored or preferred." *Wallace*, 472 U.S. at 70. Congress cannot pass laws that aid religions "based on a belief in the existence of God as against those religions founded on different beliefs." *Wallace*, 472 U.S. at 55. Thus, government endorsement of a religion or disapproval of a religion is unconstitutional. *County of Allegheny*, 492 U.S. at 593–594; *see also Lynch*, 465 U.S. at 689 (O'Connor, J., concurring).

9. Critique this paradigm. (It stops before the application.)

Mary's website is transformative of the show *Bold* because it presents the show's material in a new form. A use is transformative if it adds something new to the original with a further purpose or different character, altering the original with new expression, meaning, or message. *Campbell v. Acuff-Rose*, 510 U.S. 569, 579 (1994); see also *Blanch v. Koons*, 467 F.3d 244, 251–52 (2d Cir. 2006) (does the secondary use add value to the original?); *American Geophysical Union v. Texaco, Inc.*, 60 F.3d 913, 923 (2d Cir. 1994) ("The 'transformative use' concept is pertinent to a court's investigation under the first factor because it assesses the value generated by the secondary use and the means by which such value is generated."). In other words, the new work should not merely supersede the objects of the original. *Campbell*, 510 U.S. at 579.

In *Warner Bros. Entertainment, Inc. v. RDR Books*, 575 F. Supp. 2d 513 (S.D.N.Y. 2008), a court held a Harry Potter Lexicon book to be transformative because it served as a reference work. The author's purpose in writing the book was "to create an encyclopedia that collected and organized information from the Harry Potter books in one central source for fans to use for reference." *Id.* In analyzing the lexicon, the court stated, "Presumably, Rowling created the Harry Potter series for the expressive purpose of telling an entertaining and thought-provoking story centered on the character Harry Potter and set in a magical world. The Lexicon, on the other hand, uses material from the series for the practical purpose of making information about the intricate world of Harry Potter readily accessible to readers in a reference guide." *Id.* The court concluded, "Because it serves these reference purposes, rather than the entertainment or aesthetic purposes of the original works, the lexicon's use is transformative and does not supplant the objects of the Harry Potter works." *Id.*

10. Critique the following paradigm. (It is the first paragraph of the paradigm.)

Mary's website is transformative of the show *Bold* because it presents the show's material in a new form. It adds something new to the original in that it includes her drawings of the show, discussions of the characters, a discussion of the show's themes, and biographies of the show's stars, all of which alter the original with new expression and meaning. In addition, it has a different purpose than the original. A use is transformative if it adds something new to the original with a further purpose or different character, altering the original with new expression, meaning, or message. *Campbell v. Acuff-Rose*, 510 U.S. 569, 579 (1994); see also *Blanch v. Koons*, 467 F.3d 244, 251–52 (2d

Cir. 2006) (does the secondary use add value to the original?); *American Geophysical Union v. Texaco, Inc.*, 60 F.3d 913, 923 (2d Cir. 1994) ("The 'transformative use' concept is pertinent to a court's investigation under the first factor because it assesses the value generated by the secondary use and the means by which such value is generated."). In other words, the new work should not merely supersede the objects of the original. *Campbell*, 510 U.S. at 579. As one court has stated, "Rather than making some contribution of new intellectual value and thereby fostering the advancement of the arts and sciences, an untransformed copy is likely to be used simply for the same intrinsic purpose as the original, thereby providing limited justification for a finding of fair use." *American Geophysical*, 510 U.S. at 923. Transformative works lie at "the heart of the fair use doctrine's guarantee of breathing space within the confines of copyright" because they further the goal of copyright—to promote science and the arts. *Campbell*, 510 U.S. at 579. On the other hand, an untransformed use usually has the same intrinsic purpose as the original, limiting any justification for fair use. *American Geophysical*, 510 U.S. at 923.

Answers

1. The paradigm lacks a rule explanation. Giving your reader a couple of rule illustrations is not enough; your reader needs a full rule explanation to completely understand the law.

2. The comparison lacks an application of the law to the facts; it only contains case comparisons. Corrected version:

Mary's website is transformative because it adds something new to the original in that it includes her drawings of the show, discussions of the characters, a discussion of the show's themes, and biographies of the show's stars, all of which alter the original with new expression and meaning. It has a different purpose than the original. *Bold*'s purpose is entertainment, while Mary's website is informative. The website does not supersede the original; rather, it helps explain the show. Because it adds to the original, the website satisfies the purpose of copyright in advancing the arts and the sciences.

3. The first problem is that the paradigm starts with an issue rather than a conclusion. While many legal writers start a paradigm with an issue, it is stronger and clearer to start with the conclusion. The other problem is that the sentences in the rule explanation need to be in a more logical order. Corrected version:

> In other words, the new work should not merely supersede the objects of the original. *Campbell*, 510 U.S. at 579. Transformative works lie at "the heart of the fair use doctrine's guarantee of breathing space within the confines of copyright" because they further the goal of copyright—to promote science and the arts. *Id.* On the other hand, an untransformed use usually has the same intrinsic purpose as the original, limiting any justification for fair use. *American Geophysical*, 510 U.S. at 923.

4. First, the rule illustration begins with the facts of the case. Starting with the facts does not give the reader any context. Always start a rule illustration with the case's holding as it relates to the issue or subissue of the section. Next, I would like to see a little more detail, especially of the case's reasoning. Finally, the example could use some editing for wordiness (e.g., "reasoned this statute to violate").

5. There isn't any application of the law to the facts in this example; it is just case comparison. You need both application of the law to the facts and case comparison to create a convincing analysis.

6. The example needs a better topic sentence. The last sentence would have been better as the topic sentence. Also, this could use some editing. In particular, I would eliminate "clearly" and "plainly." These words do not make your argument stronger. Rather, they make it appear that you don't have much to back up your argument.

7. This one makes me cringe because of the two uses of "extremely" and overuse of conclusory statements. It needs a more detailed comparison to be convincing, and it lacks any comparison of the cases' reasoning.

8. Where is the rule? It is the last sentence in this paragraph. It should be the second sentence. Otherwise, you are putting the explanation before the rule.

9. This exercise contains a conclusion, a rule, a rule explanation, and a rule illustration, with everything in the proper order. The problem is that the rule explanation is too short. A reader will usually need more than one sentence of rule explanation to understand the rule.

10. The paragraph puts application of the law to the facts before presenting the law. The reader will not understand the application until she understands the law. Save the second and third sentences for the application section.

Counterargument and the Small-Scale Paradigm

Counterargument is an important part of legal writing. You can place counterargument in three places: (1) as a separate section, 2) after the small-scale paradigm for each issue or subissue, or 3) as part of the small-scale paradigm. I will discuss the last two in this chapter.

A writer will often put a counterargument after the small-scale paradigm for each section or subsection. As I will discuss in the next chapter, the best way to organize a brief is to use a small-scale paradigm for each issue or subissue. In other words, a brief will consist of several paradigms (mini analyses). In this instance, a good place to put counterargument is after the small-scale paradigm for the issue, subissue, or sub-subissue.

Example
Small-Scale Paradigm
Counterargument

This location for counterargument works well because it puts the argument and counterargument together, rather than separating them, which allows the reader to forget the details of the positive argument. It also gives the writer a psychological advantage because the reader sees the positive argument first, which weakens the other side's argument even before the reader has reached it. This placement also permits the writer to fully develop the counterargument.

Another place to put counterargument is within the small-scale paradigm. You can put counterargument in either the rule application section or case comparison section of the application. A rule application usually shows how a rule or part of a rule applies to the facts of the case. On the other hand, you might want to show that the rule doesn't apply to the facts of the brief. This fits well in the rule application (application of the law to the facts) of the paradigm.

Example

Conclusion
Law
    Rule
    Rule Explanation
    Rule Illustration
Application
    Apply the Rule (show that the law—rule and rule explanation—does not apply to your facts)
    Compare Cases

You may want to distinguish a case, that is, show that the facts of the precedent case are not like the facts of your case, to argue that the court should not apply the precedent case rule to your case. You can do this with the rule illustration and case comparison sections of the paradigm. You would illustrate a case in the rule illustration section, then distinguish that case in the case comparison section. A particularly effective way to use this structure is to have two cases in the rule illustration section, then show how case one is like your case in the case comparison section, and how case two is not like your case.

Example

Conclusion
Law
    Rule

        Rule Explanation
        Rule Illustration
            Case A
            Case B
    Application
        Apply the Rule
        Compare Cases
            Case A (show similarity)
            Case B (distinguish)

I have given you an example of how this works above (case comparison that distinguishes the rule illustration).

Conclusion

In conclusion, using a small-scale paradigm like the one I have presented in this chapter can help you organize your writing and make your writing more readable for your reader. However, you should not force something into the small-scale paradigm that does not fit. You should always let your material dictate the organization.

Chapter 8

Large- and Medium-Scale Organization

Chapter Goals

1. To help you understand the importance of large- and medium-scale organization.
2. To help you prepare an outline.
3. To help you organize a legal argument or a discussion section.
4. To help you understand how to articulate the structure of a document.
5. To help you organize other types of documents.
6. To help you create continuity between sections, subsections, and paragraphs.

Large- and medium-scale organization is as important as organization of the sentence and paragraph. A paper that lacks a clear and coherent large- and medium-scale structure is difficult to read and understand. A well-structured paper guides the reader through the paper like an evenly flowing river, taking the reader gently from subject to subject. The paper's content should generate the structure; the writer should not force a structure on a paper. A coherent paper generally falls into clear sections and subsections.

After having done some research (and reflection), but before beginning to write, the author should draft an outline. He or she does not have to adhere faithfully to the outline in the final version, but developing an outline before writing helps create a well-structured paper. The first step in preparing an outline is to carefully review the paper's purpose. What problems are you writing about? Who is the intended audience? Are you writing an argumentative paper or an explanatory one? What are the subtopics? How do they fit together? What are your conclusions?

Organization of a Discussion or Argument Section

A lawyer will generally use the law to organize the discussion section of an objective memorandum or the argument section of a brief. When there are two or more issues, you should organize using the issues. You should put the issues in a logical order. Possibilities for organizing issues include (1) put threshold issues first, (2) put the issues in order of cause of action, or (3) put most important issues first. Consider the following examples.

1. This court should grant the defendant's motion to dismiss based on lack of personal jurisdiction.
2. A plaintiff cannot recover for negligent infliction of emotional harm.

1. The defendant owed a duty to the plaintiff.
2. The defendant breached the duty owed to the plaintiff.
3. The defendant's conduct caused the plaintiff's damages.
4. The plaintiff incurred damages.

When there is only one issue or within an issue, organize by the law. In other words, take the relevant rule, break it into parts, subparts, and so on. You should not force subdivisions. When you can't subdivide anymore, use the small-scale paradigm from the previous chapter.

First, you need to find the relevant rule for the section. You can do this by (1) using a rule already synthesized by a case, (2) synthesizing a rule from several cases, (3) basing a rule on a statute or administrative rule, or (4) synthesizing a rule from a statute and cases. If you use an already synthesized rule, you should make certain that it is up to date and the best statement of the rule.

Example: Negligence

I. Duty
II. Breach of Duty
    A. First factual proof
    B. Second factual proof
III. Causation
    A. Causation-in-fact
    B. Proximate cause
        1. First factual proof
        2. Second factual proof
IV. Damages

Here, the argument is on negligence. I broke the body into four parts because the negligence rule has four parts. I broke down breach of duty because I have two ways of proving breach of duty. I broke causation into two parts because there are two types of causation: causation-in-fact and proximate cause. I broke proximate cause into two parts because I have two ways of establishing proximate cause.

Assume that in your jurisdiction intentional infliction of emotional harm consists of four elements: (1) outrageous conduct by the defendant, (2) intentional conduct by the defendant, (3) that causes, (4) the plaintiff severe emotional distress. You would outline a discussion section or argument section based on this rule by dividing it into four parts, based on the parts of the rule. You would then divide each part into subparts, based on how the rule breaks down in relation to your case. For example, you might break down section I into two parts based on the fact that you have two different ways to satisfy this element. You would similarly break down section III. I broke section IV into three subparts.

Example: Intentional Infliction of Emotional Harm

I. Outrageous Conduct
    A. First factual proof

B. Second factual proof
II. Intentional Conduct
III. Causation
    A. First factual proof
    B. Second factual proof
IV. Severe Emotional Distress
    A. First factual proof
    B. Second factual proof
    C. Third factual proof

Next, you should modify the outline based on what is actually at issue in your facts.

Example: Intentional Infliction of Emotional Harm

I. Outrageous Conduct
    A. First factual proof
    B. Second factual proof
II. Causation
    A. First factual proof
    B. Second factual proof
III. Severe Emotional Distress
    A. First factual proof
    B. Second factual proof
    C. Third factual proof

I removed the original II (intentional conduct) because it was not in dispute in my hypothetical. You should still mention all the elements of a rule in the introduction.

When the rule cannot be broken down further, you should use the small-scale paradigm from the previous chapter to organize the sections and subsections.

In many cases, the law you will use to organize a discussion or argument section will be a statute. You should use the same principles for organizing a discussion or argument based on a statute as you did above. Break down the statute into its main parts, then keep subdividing as far as is logical.

Make an outline based on the above. Using the outline, determine which parts and subparts are in controversy. Eliminate those parts that are not in controversy, then use the rest as your organization.

Example: Fair Use Statute (Copyright)

Notwithstanding the provisions of sections 106 and 106A, the fair use of a copyrighted work, including such use by reproduction in copies or phonorecords or by any other means specified by that section, for purposes such as criticism, comment, news reporting, teaching (including multiple copies for classroom use), scholarship, or research, is not an infringement of copyright. In determining whether the use made of a work in any particular case is a fair use, the factors to be considered shall include:

(1) the purpose and character of the use, including whether such use is of a commercial nature or is for nonprofit educational purposes;

(2) the nature of the copyrighted work;

(3) the amount and substantiality of the portion used in relation to the copyrighted work as a whole; and

(4) the effect of the use upon the potential market for or value of the copyrighted work.

The fact that a work is unpublished shall not itself bar a finding of fair use if such finding is made upon consideration of all the above factors.

I would outline the statute as follows.

Introduction

A. Notwithstanding the provisions of sections 106 and 106A, [reference]

B. the fair use of a copyrighted work . . . is not an infringement of copyright, [main rule]

C. including such use by reproduction in copies or phonorecords or by any other means specified by that section, for purposes such as criticism, comment, news reporting, or teaching (including multiple copies for classroom use). [examples]

Body

In determining whether the use made of a work in any particular case is a fair use the factors to be considered shall include—

I. the purpose and character of the use, including whether such use
  A. is of a commercial nature or
  B. is for nonprofit educational purposes;
II. the nature of the copyrighted work;
III. the amount and substantiality of the portion used in relation to the copyrighted work as a whole; and
  A. the amount
  B. the substantiality
IV. the effect of the use upon the potential market for or value of the copyrighted work.
  A. potential market for
  B. value of

Clarification

The fact that a work is unpublished shall not itself bar a finding of fair use if such finding is made upon consideration of all the above factors.

After having carefully read the statute and reviewed my facts, I concluded that I wanted to organize the body of my argument by the four fair use factors above so the body consisted of four parts. I also discovered that courts have added a subfactor (transformative or nontransformative), so I added it to my organization. (Cases will often add subsections or sub-subsections to your outline because they define the broad meaning of the statute.)

Assuming that all factors and subfactors are in dispute, my outline would be:

I. Purpose and Character of the Use
  A. commercial nature or nonprofit education purpose
  B. transformative or nontransformative
II. Nature of the Copyrighted Work
III. Amount and Substantiality

A. amount
B. substantiality
IV. Effect of the Use
A. potential market
B. value of

Of course, most of the time, all the factors and subfactors will not be in controversy, or you may not argue a factor or subfactor because of strategy (e.g., the argument is not worth taking up valuable space).

Example: Fair Use
I. Purpose and Character of the Use
A. commercial nature or nonprofit education purpose
B. transformative or nontransformative
II. Amount and Substantiality
A. amount
B. substantiality
III. Effect (Value of) the Use

Exercise 8-1

1. Look at the argument sections of several briefs you have recently written. Are they well organized on the large- and medium-scale levels? Did you organize them based on the law? How could you have organized them better?
2. Look at the argument sections of other briefs. Are they well organized? Could you outline them easily? Are they organized by the law? How could you have organized them better?

> ## Pointers
>
> 1. Always create an outline before you begin to write.
> 2. Organize the discussion section or argument of documents with multiple issues by putting the issues in a logical order. Could you explain to someone else why you put the issues in that order?
> 3. With single-issue discussions or within issues, organize by the law. Break the outline down as much as you can, without going too far. Leave out any sections or subsections that are not in dispute. When you can't break down the outline any further, use the small-scale paradigm.

Articulating the Organization

Articulating the organization of the discussion section or argument section helps your reader. You can articulate the large- and medium-scale organization with introductions, headings and subheadings, thesis paragraphs, closure devices, and conclusions.

There is a common saying among writing teachers that writers should tell the reader what they are going to say, tell them, then tell them what they said. The "tell them what you are going to say" part refers to introductions and thesis paragraphs. Introductions and thesis paragraphs are important because they introduce the reader to the organization of the section or subsection. They also create repetition so that the reader is more likely to remember the ideas. Headings and subheadings help the reader with the organization of the "tell them" part. Finally, conclusions are the "tell them what you just said." Readers need a wrap-up.

Introduction

An introduction sets up the sections and subsections. It usually includes the rule, sets the context, and includes material that doesn't belong under the headings. You should carefully organize the introduction. It should reflect the organization of the body of the discussion or argument. In other words, it serves as a road map to guide your reader through the discussion or argument. It should also follow the general principles for organizing any legal discussion or argument: conclusion, law, application (analysis). Here is an example of the main part of the introduction.

> Reciting the Pledge of Allegiance with the words "under God" in a public classroom violates the Establishment Clause of the 1st Amendment of the United States Constitution. [←overall conclusion] [law→] This Court has created a three-part test to evaluate Establishment Clause questions: (1) the practice must have a secular purpose, (2) the principal or primary effect of the practice must neither advance nor inhibit religion, and (3) the practice must not give rise to excessive entanglement between government and religion. *Cite.* [conclusion concerning test→] Reciting the Pledge with the words "under God" violates all of these factors. [analysis issue one→] First, there is no secular purpose in including the words "under God" in the Pledge of Allegiance. The Pledge fully conveys its patriotic meaning without those words. [analysis issue two→] Second, the principal or primary effect of the practice advances religion because it tells the listener that those who believe in a monotheistic deity are favored by the government. [analysis issue three→] Finally, the practice excessively entangles the government in religion because the school must monitor those who do not want to participate. Moreover, reciting the Pledge causes excessive governmental entanglement because reciting the Pledge with the words "under God" creates political divisiveness. [Other introductory material that does not belong in the body of the argument, such as the standard of review.]

The above introduction is well organized. It clearly sets out the three parts of the test. It then applies the parts of the test to the facts in order. Based on this introduction, I would assume that the body of the argument falls into three parts.

You can also intertwine brief policy arguments into the introduction.

Goodwill is one of the most valuable assets of a franchisor. If the quality of the food and service is high and the prices reasonable, customers will frequently return to the franchise; but if the food is poor, the service is slow, or the prices are too high, business will suffer. The goodwill of a nationwide franchise depends on the quality of its franchisees. If a customer gets a bad meal at a franchisee's restaurant, he or she may assume that this will happen at other outlets in the chain. Thus, a franchisor must be able to terminate those franchises that do not meet the franchiser's standards.

Scholarly papers also have their own practices. The introduction of a scholarly paper generally ends as in the following example.

Part II of this paper will discuss concepts of copyright property in the 19th century in order to provide a basis of comparison for examination of copyright property in the 20th century. Part III will show how certain 19th-century concepts of property—the natural rights basis of property and the physicalist view of property—broke down in the early 20th century and were replaced by new concepts. Part IV will explore the vast expansion of the subject matter of copyright in the first half of the 20th century, which significantly enlarged the scope of copyright property.

The right of free speech, guaranteed by the First Part V will deal with what copyright protects and does not protect. It will first discuss the Hohfeldian view of property as a set of legal relations. It will next examine a copyright holder's statutory rights and the courts' expansion of those rights. It will then cover the economic basis of copyright protection, the ordinary observer test of copyright infringement, the amount taken, the idea–expression dichotomy in copyright law, the requirement of originality, and limitations on copyright, including fair use. Part VI will examine *International News Service v. Associated Press*, which demonstrates the two major 20th-century bases of property: property as exchange value and property as a creation of the state based on public policy.

Exercise 8-2

1. Look at some briefs you have recently written. Do they contain well-organized introductions that set up the sections and subsections of the body of the argument? Can you label the parts of your introductions? How could you improve your introductions?
2. Look at a few briefs written by others. Do they contain well-organized introductions that set up the sections and subsections of the body of the argument? Can you label the parts of the introductions? How could you improve the introductions?

Headings and Subheadings

Headings and subheadings tell the reader what is in the section or subsection. They are road signs to help your reader navigate your discussion, argument, or other writing. They should be full sentences, and they should be as specific as possible so that the reader will know what the section or subsection concerns. Headings and subheadings in an objective memo should be positive statements or questions. You should base them on the issue or subissue, and they should include both the law and the facts. Headings and subsections in an argument section (point headings) should be arguments. They should generally contain the conclusion, the law, the facts, and the reasoning (because). Here are some examples:

1. Did Mr. Johnson establish minimum contacts with Alabama when he signed a contract with an Alabama company? (objective)
2. Mr. Johnson established minimum contacts with Alabama when he signed a contract with an Alabama company. (objective)
3. The court has personal jurisdiction over Mr. Johnson because he established minimum contacts with Alabama when he signed a contract with an Alabama company. (persuasive)
4. The defendant breached a duty owed to the defendant when he texted on his cell phone because texting diverted his attention from the road and caused the accident. (persuasive)

5. Having a menorah on the courthouse steps violates the Establishment Clause because there is no secular purpose in having a menorah there. (persuasive)

In creating headings, one should use different numbering or lettering systems, sizes, type styles, capitalization, and placement to distinguish the heading levels. For example, section headings might be preceded by a roman numeral, be centered, be in bold, and have all letters capitalized. First-level subsections might be preceded by a capital letter, be centered, be underlined, and have the first letter of important words capitalized. Second-level subsections might be preceded by a number, be flush left, be in regular type, and have only the first word capitalized. In using headings, one should pay attention to the page's look.[1] Also, headings and subheadings should not be too long; headings and subheadings should rarely exceed three lines.

Exercise 8-3

Critique these headings.

1. Did the court have personal jurisdiction over the defendant? (objective)
2. The court did not have subject matter jurisdiction over Mr. Chin because both Mr. Chin and Mr. Armstrong were citizens of South Carolina. (persuasive)
3. The parties did not enter into a contract. (persuasive)
4. Did the parties create a contract when Mr. Hernandez sent his acceptance two minutes after the deadline stated in the offer? (objective)
5. Summary judgment should be granted by the court because the offer stated that Mr. Hernandez must accept it before midnight on September 24th and there is no dispute that Mr. Hernandez accepted the offer after that time. (persuasive)

---

1. Of course, the same applies to other factors that affect a page's look, including margins, typeface, page number placement, and paper quality.

6. The decedent's will was not valid because it did not meet the statutory requirements. (persuasive)

7. The decedent's will was not valid because it did not meet the statutory requirement of the signing by the testator being witnessed by two witnesses, and, while one witness was in the room at the time of the signing, the other witness was in the next room taking a cell phone call from his wife, although he could see the signing from there. (persuasive)

8. Mr. Franklin lacked minimum contacts with Florida. (persuasive)

9. Mr. Hernandez accepted the contract after the time set forth in the offer. (persuasive)

10. Mr. Hernandez accepted the contract after the time set forth in the offer. (objective)

Answers

1. A good heading needs more detail. You should include the facts.

2. This is a good point heading because it contains all the elements needed for a persuasive heading. It contains the conclusion, the law, the facts, and the why.

3. This is not a good point heading because it contains only the conclusion.

4. This is a good heading because it gives the reader the exact issue.

5. This heading contains all the elements of a good point heading. However, it is in the passive voice. Read the heading out loud. Using the passive voice here subtracts from the persuasiveness of the heading.

6. More detail would help the reader here. What statutory requirement did the will lack?

7. This one is just a little too long. While details are important, headings should be readable the first time through.

8. The writer has omitted the conclusion, so this is not a persuasive heading. What is the consequence of not having minimum contacts with Florida? Moreover, it lacks detailed facts and a detailed why.

9. Again, there is no conclusion. The heading includes detailed facts, but it does not state the consequences of those facts.

10. An objective heading should include the law.

Thesis Paragraphs

Thesis paragraphs introduce the subsections.[2] You should put thesis paragraphs before subdivisions, and they should reflect the organization of the subsections. They set the context for a section and summarize what the section is going to discuss. You can consider them mini introductions or mini road maps.

> This paper's thesis is that a universal system of basic rights is hardwired into our brains (a universal grammar of rights), just like morality is hardwired into our brains. In fact, rights relate to our innate ability to tell right from wrong. Like morality, our hardwired rights are general principles, with the details of these rights being specified by particular cultures. In other words, we have an innate toolkit for building a system of rights. Among these rights are (1) property rights, (2) a right to basic fairness, (3) liberty rights, and (4) a right to be treated equally. These innate rights are not a minimum, but rather a foundation.

(Note how this example starts with a strong topic sentence, which sets out the topic of the section.)

In legal writing, the thesis paragraph usually sets out the problem, presents the applicable rule, applies the rule to the facts, and gives the writer's conclusions.

> I. Was Mr. Smith's Conduct of Shouting a Common Obscenity at Mrs. Davis Outrageous?
> The first issue in this case is whether Smith's conduct constitutes outrageous conduct. In *Owens*, the court stated that outrageous conduct must shock the conscience. Smith's conduct in this case involved shouting a common obscenity at Mrs. Davis. Such conduct does not involve outrageous conduct.

Here's an annotated example:

---

2. You don't need a thesis paragraph when there are no subdivisions.

I. The Adhesion Contract Is Unconscionable Because Mrs. Walters Lacked Meaningful Choice and the Terms Were Unreasonably in Favor of the Car Dealer

The adhesion contract in this case is unconscionable. [←overall conclusion] Courts have defined unconscionability as an absence of meaningful choice on the part of one of the parties together with contract terms, which are unreasonably favorable to the other party. *Cite.* [←law] [application issue one→] In this case, Mrs. Walters lacked a meaningful choice because all of the defendant's competitors had contracts with the same terms, and she was an individual dealing with a large corporation. [application issue two→] Similarly, the contracts terms were unreasonably favorable to the defendant because the company could repossess her car if she was late with a single payment.

Based on the thesis paragraph, I would assume that there are two subsections (with subheadings) because there are two main parts to the rule. Notice how the paragraph follows the standard organization for a legal argument: conclusion, law, application.

A thesis paragraph will generally reflect the structure of the section or subsection that it introduces.

I. Does a federal district court have subject matter jurisdiction over a defendant when no federal question is involved and when the amount in controversy is less than the statutory minimum and the parties are citizens of the same state?

The federal district court does not have subject matter jurisdiction over this matter. First, no federal question is involved. This suit concerns only state law tort issues. Second, the court lacks diversity jurisdiction over the suit. The amount in controversy is less than the statutory minimum; at most, damages comprise $10,000. Similarly, both the plaintiff and defendant are citizens of North Carolina. The plaintiff's domicile is Durham, and the defendant's principal place of business is Raleigh. Accordingly, this court will probably grant the defendant's motion to dismiss.

There are two main divisions in the preceding: federal question jurisdiction and diversity jurisdiction. The second section probably falls into two subparts: amount in controversy and diversity of citizenship. (You can assume that the section or subsection is organized like the thesis paragraph.) Always remember it is the writer's job to help the reader understand what she has written.

Exercise 8-4

Find an article in a magazine or an essay in a book, and analyze how the author organizes the thesis paragraphs. Examine how the thesis paragraphs help organize sections and subsections.

Do you use thesis paragraphs in your memorandums and briefs? If you don't, can you see how they help the reader understand your organization better? Take a brief you have recently written and add thesis paragraphs. Examine them to see if they are effective in introducing the ideas and organization of the sections. Label the parts of the thesis paragraphs.

Closure

Closure helps articulate a paper's structure. Sections and subsections should come to a definite end. You can do this by clearly and logically organizing each section and by putting conclusions or summaries at the end of a section when necessary. The need for closure does not prevent you from providing transitions between sections and subsections, but the breaks between sections and subsections should be clear.

Exercise 8-5

Look at a document you have recently written. Is there closure at the end of sections and subsections?

Conclusion

The conclusion sums up the body of the discussion or argument section. If the discussion or argument section consists of three main sections, your conclusion should generally comprise four sentences: overall conclusion, conclusion I, conclusion II, conclusion III. You can add additional sentences for additional subsections. In a persuasive document you can also tell the court what it should do. (Use "should," not "must.") A conclusion should generally not include new material.

> The above has demonstrated that there has been no false imprisonment in this case. For the plaintiff to recover for false imprisonment, she must satisfy all three elements of the test. While she might have satisfied the first two elements, she did not satisfy the last one as a matter of law. The defendant was not conscious of the confinement because she testified that she was not aware the door to the manager's office was locked. Consequently, this court should reverse the lower court's decision.

Note: I did not specifically discuss the first two elements of false imprisonment in the conclusion because I would have mentioned them in the introduction and because they are not important to the outcome to the case.

Exercise 8-6

1. Look at several briefs you have recently written. Do they contain clear, well-organized conclusions? Do they include unnecessary material?
2. Look at a few briefs written by others. Do they contain clear, well-organized conclusions? Could you have written them better?

Bringing It Together

Here is an outline of an argument section, which includes all the ways to articulate the structure.

Introduction
I. Heading
   Thesis Paragraph
   A. Subheading
   B. Subheading
II. Heading
III. Heading
   Thesis Paragraph
   A. Subheading
   B. Subheading
   C. Subheading
      Thesis Paragraph
      1. Sub-subheading
      2. Sub-subheading
IV. Heading
Conclusion

A thesis paragraph is not necessary under II and IV because there are no subdivisions.

Some of my students have told me that having introductions, thesis paragraphs, headings and subheadings, and conclusions produces too much repetition. I reply to them that the repetition is necessary because the reader is reading your brief for the first time. You want your reader to understand your arguments with the least amount of effort as is possible. Of course, you don't want your conclusion to read exactly like your introduction; use elegant variation.

Here is how you relate the large- and medium-scale organization of this chapter with the small-scale organization of the previous one.

Introduction

I. Heading
    Thesis Paragraph
    A. Subheading
    Small-Scale Paradigm
    B. Subheading
    Small-Scale Paradigm
II. Heading
Small-Scale Paradigm
III. Heading
    Thesis Paragraph
    A. Subheading
    Small-Scale Paradigm
    B. Subheading
    Small-Scale Paradigm
    C. Subheading
        Thesis Paragraph
        1. Sub-subheading
        Small-Scale Paradigm
        2. Sub-subheading
        Small-Scale Paradigm
IV. Heading
Small-Scale Paradigm
Conclusion

Do you see how the parts fit together? If you don't, review Chapters 7 and 8.

<table>
<tr><td colspan="2">**Pointers**</td></tr>
<tr><td>1.</td><td>Help your readers understand the organization of your argument section or discussion section by using introductions, headings, thesis paragraphs, and conclusions.</td></tr>
<tr><td>2.</td><td>An introduction should set up the issues and subissues. It should be well organized. You should be able to label every sentence of the main part of the introduction as conclusion, law, or application.</td></tr>
<tr><td>3.</td><td>Use headings and subheadings to help your reader understand your organization and to introduce the topic of the section or subsection. Objective headings and subheadings should be positive statements or questions, and they should include both the law and the facts. Point headings and subheadings should usually contain the conclusion, the law, the facts, and the reasoning.</td></tr>
<tr><td>4.</td><td>Use thesis paragraphs to set up sections and subsections. Thesis paragraphs should follow the organization of the section or subsection. You should be able to label the main sentences of thesis paragraphs as conclusion, law, or facts.</td></tr>
<tr><td>5.</td><td>Use conclusions to sum up your evaluation or argument. The conclusion should reflect the organization of the body of the discussion or argument.</td></tr>
</table>

Other Types of Medium- and Large-Scale Organization

A lawyer will also write other types of documents, such as client letters, fact sections of objective memorandums and briefs, articles, and so on that cannot use the small-scale paradigm or the methods of large- and medium-scale organization presented in the previous sections. The key to organizing other types of writings is to let the material dictate the organization. As stated above, always draft an outline before you start writing.

One can use many of the same organizations on the medium- and large-scale levels that are used for paragraphs. These include topical organization, chronological organization, spatial organization, climactic organization, inductive or deductive structures, analogical structure, and free-form organization based on the material. These structures are particularly useful for the organizations of sections. Please review these organizations from the previous chapters. A common type of organization is introduction, expository paragraphs, conclusion.

Exercise 8-7

Reorganize this statement of facts from an objective memorandum.

In response to a termination notice, plaintiff filed suit in federal district court, claiming that defendant had attempted to fix prices, conspired with other area franchisees to fix prices and restrain trade, and tried to create a monopoly under §§ 1 and 2 of the Sherman Antitrust Act. Plaintiff operates its restaurants under a standard franchise agreement. The agreement provides that the franchisor may terminate the franchise for failure to operate in accordance with standards, for not operating as to maximize profits of all parties, and for conduct that may detract from the value of the Captain Hook trademark. If a violation occurs, the franchisor must give written notice of the violation to the franchisee. If the violation is not corrected within thirty days, the franchisor may terminate the franchise and the franchisee must cease operations and remove all references to the Captain Hook trademark within 10 days.

Defendant sent a 30-day notice to the plaintiff stating that it would terminate the plaintiff's franchises if it did not bring its operations up to standard and lower its prices to competitive levels. Customers had made numerous complaints to plaintiff involving the quality of the stores. The complaints stated that the food was often cold, that trash was not cleaned up in the dining area, and that the lighting was poor in the parking lot. In addition, the plaintiff had been charging prices well above other Garden City outlets and had recently raised prices on certain items to 30 percent above those charged by other area stores. Business at plaintiff's restaurants has dropped 20 percent in recent months.

Captain Hook's Seafood, Inc. (the "defendant") is the franchisor of Captain Hook's Seafood Restaurants. It both franchises stores and owns them. Captain Hook's of Garden City, Hysteria, Inc. (the "plaintiff') operates four of defendant's restaurants in Garden City, Hysteria. Defendant owns three restaurants in Garden City, and another franchisee one more. The eight restaurants do not compete with each other because they are in different parts of Garden City.

The issue in this case is whether defendant's termination of plaintiff's franchise for not operating according to defendant's standards and not operating as to maximize profits violates § 1 or § 2 of the Sherman Antitrust Act.

Answer

The issue in this case is whether defendant's termination of plaintiff's franchise for not operating according to defendant's standards and not operating as to maximize profits violates § 1 or § 2 of the Sherman Antitrust Act. Captain Hook's Seafood, Inc. (the "defendant") is the franchisor of Captain Hook's Seafood Restaurants. It both franchises stores and owns them. Captain Hook's of Garden City, Hysteria, Inc. (the "plaintiff') operates four of defendant's restaurants in Garden City, Hysteria. Defendant owns three restaurants in Garden City, and another franchisee one more. The eight restaurants do not compete with each other because they are in different parts of Garden City.

Plaintiff operates its restaurants under a standard franchise agreement. The agreement provides that the franchisor may terminate the franchise for failure to operate in accordance with standards, for not operating as to maximize profits of all parties, and for conduct that may detract from the value of the Captain Hook trademark. If a violation occurs, the franchisor must give written notice of the violation to the franchisee. If the violation is not corrected within 30 days, the franchisor may terminate the franchise and the franchisee must cease operations and remove all reference to the Captain Hook trademark within 10 days.

Defendant sent a 30–day notice to the plaintiff stating that it would terminate the plaintiff's franchises if it did not bring its operations up to standard and lower its prices to competitive levels. Customers had made numerous complaints to plaintiff involving the quality of the stores. The complaints stated that the food was often cold, that trash was not cleaned up in the dining area, and that the lighting was poor in the parking lot. In addition, the plaintiff had been charging prices well above other Garden City outlets and had recently raised prices on certain items to 30 percent above those charged by other area stores. Business at plaintiff's restaurants has dropped 20 percent in recent months.

In response to the termination notice, plaintiff filed suit in federal district court, claiming that defendant had attempted to fix prices, conspired with other area franchisees to fix prices and restrain trade, and tried to create a monopoly under §§ 1 and 2 of the Sherman Antitrust Act.

The original statement of facts is not in a logical order. The original gives important information before the context is set.

I like to start the statement of facts with a clear statement of what the case involves to give the reader context. Next, I usually introduce the parties so that the reader understands the relationship of the parties. Then, I give the material facts in chronological order. In writing up the facts, it is generally best to tell a story. Finally, I end with the procedure.

Pointers

1. You should logically organize everything you write on the large- and medium-scale levels.
2. You should be able to explain the logic behind your organization if someone asks.
3. If you can't outline it, you have not organized it logically.

Creating Continuity and Flow Between Paragraphs, Subsections, and Sections

As was true of sentences in a paragraph, the writer needs to create continuity and flow between paragraphs, subsections, and sections. One way of doing this is to think in large blocks. How do the paragraphs fit together within a section? How do the paragraphs relate? Do the ideas progress in a logical order? Are the more important ideas emphasized? Do the paragraphs seem to flow together? Is there a continuity of style within a subsection or section? Do all the paragraphs relate to the thesis paragraph? Do all the paragraphs relate to the heading or subheading?

Again, the best tool to test continuity and flow is reading the paper aloud. You should read the paper as if it were poetry or a novel, rather than dry prose. Carefully listen to your voice, particularly the rising and falling of tone and the lengths of the pauses caused by punctuation.

Relating all the paragraphs in a section or subsection to the thesis paragraphs and the heading or subheading helps create continuity. Each paragraph should introduce a new subtopic. If a paragraph seems out of place, the author should rewrite it, move it to another section, or delete it.

Creating a hierarchy also helps create coherence and flow. The writer should emphasize important ideas and subordinate supporting material. As stated in Chapter 4, placement is the main tool for creating emphasis. The author should put the most important ideas first or last. One can also use sentence structure to establish hierarchy, such as placing important material in independent clauses and secondary material in dependent clauses. If you are having difficulty creating a hierarchy of ideas, you could use a chart to map out your thinking.

One can also use transitional words, phrases, clauses, and sentences to create coherence and flow between paragraphs. Here are some examples of such words: in addition, moreover, next, furthermore, likewise, similarly, also, in contrast, however, on the other hand, therefore, consequently, accordingly, for example, then, although, while, and afterward.

When connecting paragraphs, use the word or phrase that best shows the relationship between the paragraphs. For example, if the paragraphs have similar ideas, you might use "similarly" or "likewise." If the paragraphs convey different ideas, you could use "in contrast" or "on the other hand." If the paragraph is illustrating an idea from a previous paragraph, you could employ "for example." If the paragraph begins a conclusion you could use "therefore" or "consequently." While this technique is a good way to connect paragraphs, if you overuse it, your writing might start to sound stilted. You should employ a variety of devices to create flow between paragraphs.

In Chapter 6, I stated that every paragraph should have a topic sentence. A topic sentence might be a transitional sentence that connects one subject to another between paragraphs. Each of these examples is the first sentence of a paragraph.

Although proving negligence might be hard for the plaintiff, establishing causation should be easier. (transitioning from a negligence subsection to a causation one)

The plaintiff can also establish defamation based on the defendant's August 23 letter. (transitioning from one way of proving defamation to another)

Second, the plaintiff can prove that the defendant breached the duty that she owed to the plaintiff. (transitioning from one element of a cause of action to another)

While it is difficult to prevent the use of pornography on the Internet by an adult, the same is not true for minors. (transitioning to an exception)

Bart, on the other hand, was a difficult child. (transitioning from a discussion of one child to another)

A writer can also use numbers to transition between ideas and to show the reader where she is in the paper. This is especially useful when discussing a cause of action that has several elements.

> The third element of intentional infliction of emotional distress is that the plaintiff's conduct must have caused the defendant's emotional distress.

> The second element of battery is that the defendant's conduct must be intentional.

Exercise 8-8

Look at an essay in a book or online.

1. Can you identify the sections and subsections? What techniques has the author used to help you understand the organization? Could you have done a better job?
2. Is there coherence between the paragraphs in sections or subsections? Do the paragraphs seem to flow from one to another? If so, how did the author create coherence and flow? Do you think that the author conceived the essay in large blocks? If the author did not do a good job of creating coherence and flow between paragraphs, can you create coherence and flow between the paragraphs?
3. Do all the paragraphs relate to the headings and thesis paragraphs? Has the author used material that is not relevant to the section or subsection?
4. Has the author created a hierarchy of important ideas and subsidiary ideas? If so, how has the author created this hierarchy?
5. Has the author used transitional words and phrases to create coherence and flow between paragraphs? If not, can you do so?
6. Has the author used enumerations to help the reader know where she is in the essay? If not, would enumerations help you better understand the essay's organization?

7. Read the essay out loud. Does this help you see the coherence and flow in the paper's various levels? Do you notice how your voice rises and falls as you read? Do you notice how you pause more at certain punctuation marks than others? Can you see how the differences in the lengths of pauses connects certain material and separates other material? Can you see how this relates to coherence and continuity?

Pointers

1. Create coherence and flow within a section by logically organizing the paragraphs.
2. Create coherence and flow by thinking in large blocks.
3. Every sentence in a paragraph should relate to the heading or subheading and the thesis paragraph.
4. Create a hierarchy of ideas by emphasizing important ideas and de-emphasizing subsidiary ones.
5. Connect paragraphs by using transitional words, phrases, and paragraphs.
6. Read your paper out loud and listen to whether you have created coherence and flow between paragraphs and subsections.

Chapter 9

Review

The previous chapters have shown you how you can improve your writing so that you can better communicate your ideas to your readers. As I have stressed throughout this book, communication is the writer's responsibility, not the reader's. The writer must remember that the reader is reading the memorandum or brief for the first time. What may seem clear to the writer, who has spent a month researching and writing a project, may not seem so clear to the reader, who is seeing the material for the first time.

As I have also stressed, the writer should always put himself in the reader's shoes. What does the reader need to know to understand your paper fully? Will the reader have any questions after finishing your paper? How can the reader criticize your arguments and conclusions?

Becoming a good writer is a lifelong endeavor. Everyone can improve their writing. A good lawyer constantly reviews her writing to determine how she can improve it. Such a lawyer effectively communicates to her colleagues, opponents, and the court. Such a lawyer effectively represents her clients, and she rarely loses cases she should win.

The Keys to Clear Legal Writing

1. Use the active voice; don't overuse the passive voice.
2. Write with verbs.
3. Avoid nominalizations whenever possible.
4. Avoid overuse of "to be" or "to have."

5. Avoid complex verb constructions.
6. Edit for wordiness.
7. Delete unnecessary repetitions.
8. Scrutinize constructions beginning with "there" or "it" for wordiness.
9. Shorten long descriptive phrases whenever possible.
10. Express the negative in positive form whenever possible.
11. Consider emphasis—sentence structure, placement, punctuation, special type.
12. Clarify lists with numbers or letters.
13. Avoid clichés and legal jargon.
14. Be specific; carefully consider the words you want to use.
15. Use demonstrative adjectives to be more specific.
16. Avoid qualifiers.
17. Combine short sentences to avoid choppiness.
18. Use a variety of sentence patterns and lengths.
19. Only combine ideas that belong together.
20. Delete redundant sentences.
21. Don't tread water.
22. Avoid overuse of particular words; use a thesaurus.
23. Avoid abrupt changes of verb tense.
24. Carefully organize paragraphs.
25. Check for paragraph unity.
26. Relate all sentences in a paragraph to the paragraph's topic sentence.
27. Use a single theme for each paragraph.
28. Use a variety of paragraph organizations.
29. Create coherence and flow.
30. Create a hierarchy of ideas, phrases, and sentences within the paragraph.
31. Think in large blocks.
32. Consider the paragraph's dynamic flow and goal.
33. Ensure each sentence flows from the previous one.
34. Consider punctuation's relation to flow. Separate linked ideas with brief punctuation (commas); separate different ideas with longer punctuation (periods and paragraph breaks).
35. Properly place primary and secondary material.

36. Use connecting words and phrases.
37. Use overlapping sentences to create continuity.
38. Repeat key words for coherence.
39. Combine short sentences to create coherence.
40. Use striking topic sentences.
41. Carefully organize the paper on medium- and large-scale levels.
42. Use the law to organize your paper.
43. Use the small-scale paradigm to organize your paper.
44. Clearly articulate subsections and sections.
45. Create closure to help articulate sections and subsections.
46. Consider the hierarchy of sections and subsections.
47. Draft an outline.
48. Organize ideas in a logical order.
49. Use headings and subheadings.
50. Set out the structure of your paper in the introduction.
51. Create continuity between paragraphs, subsections, and sections.
52. Make sure that each paragraph relates to the thesis paragraph.
53. Use transitional sentences to give a paper continuity.
54. Identify your audience.
55. Identify the constraints on the paper (format, length).
56. Edit your paper carefully.
57. Read your paper out loud and listen carefully.
58. Employ a natural writing style rather than a formal one.
59. Check the citations.
60. Carefully proofread your paper.
61. Put yourself in your reader's shoes.
62. Combine a holistic approach to writing with knowledge of the rules and mechanics of writing.

How many of the above could you have written down from memory?

Exercise 9-1

Identify the problems in the following sentences, then edit them.

1. The game was won by the Cardinals.
2. Roger Maris who was the third player to bat in the third inning hit a home run out of the park that scored three runners.
3. Her failure to pass torts was due to poor study habits.
4. Flying saucers were seen by at least 10 people.
5. Pat had to have a vacation.
6. The car went down the road quickly.
7. Sam wore a suit that was blue in color.
8. Mozart is thought to have been the greatest composer of the classical era.
9. Lesley was pretty sure she had passed the property test.
10. This court should grant the defendant's motion to dismiss because the court lacks subject matter jurisdiction, it lacks personal jurisdiction, and it is not the proper venue for the action.
11. The student's lecture was on the parole evidence rule.
12. The baseball game was canceled on account of rain.
13. The home run was hit by Roger Maris.
14. There are 12 areas the bar examiners might test us on.
15. The professor's request was that we type our papers.
16. The underground river was discovered by Sandy Smith, a famous cave explorer.
17. It is obvious that the Mets will win the pennant.
18. The editor's revisions were rather extensive.
19. James doesn't like Italian food.
20. Betty won't change jobs at this point in time.

Answers

1. The Cardinals won the game. (passive voice)
2. Roger Maris, the third player to bat in the third inning, hit a three-run homer. (wordiness)
3. She failed torts because of poor study habits. (nominalization)
4. At least 10 people saw flying saucers. (passive voice)
5. Pat needed a vacation. (complex verb form)
6. The car sped down the road. (write with verbs)
7. Sam wore a blue suit. (wordiness)

8. Mozart is considered the greatest composer of the classical era. (complex verb form)

9. Lesley was sure she had passed the property test. (use of qualifier)

10. This court should grant the defendant's motion to dismiss because (1) the court lacks subject matter jurisdiction, (2) it lacks personal jurisdiction, and (3) it is not the proper venue for the action. (clarity)

11. The student lectured on the parole evidence rule. (nominalization)

12. The baseball game was canceled due to rain. (wordiness)

13. Roger Maris hit the home run. (passive voice)

14. The bar examiners might test us on 12 areas. (wordiness)

15. The professor asked us to type our papers. (nominalization)

16. Sandy Smith, a famous cave explorer, discovered the underground river. (passive voice)

17. The Mets will win the pennant. (wordiness)

18. The editor's revisions were extensive. (use of qualifier)

19. James dislikes Italian food. (wordy negative)

20. Betty won't change jobs at this time. (wordiness)

Exercise 9-2

Rewrite the following sentences in at least three different ways to alter the emphasis.

1. John Dean, the Watergate figure, spoke at our college.
2. There is only one solution, completely rewrite the paper.
3. Jim Johnson, a rock star in the 70s, sells insurance today.
4. Although Babe Hermann, the Dodgers slugger, had hurt his knee, he could still hit with power.
5. Although Jackie had never played pool before that night, she won three games.

Answers
1. John Dean (the Watergate figure) spoke at our college.
   John Dean—the Watergate figure—spoke at our college.
   Watergate figure John Dean spoke at our college.

2. There is only one solution—completely rewrite the paper.
   There is only one solution: completely rewrite the paper.
   Completely rewriting the paper is the only solution.
3. Jim Johnson—a rock star in the 70s—sells insurance today.
   Today, Jim Johnson, a rock star in the 70s, sells insurance.
   A rock star in the 70s, Jim Johnson today sells insurance.
4. Babe Hermann, the Dodgers slugger, could still hit with power, although he had hurt his knee.
   Babe Hermann—the Dodgers slugger—could still hit with power, even though he had hurt his knee.
   Although he had hurt his knee, the Dodgers slugger Babe Hermann could still hit with power.
5. Jackie had never played pool before that night, but she won three games.
   Jackie won three games, although she had never played pool before that night.
   Despite having never played pool before that night, Jackie won three games.

Exercise 9-3

Rewrite the following sentences to make them more specific.

1. John went to the play with us.
2. The boy played with his toys.
3. The sun went down in the west.
4. The children enjoyed the concert.
5. We watched television last night.
6. I studied for the exam.
7. Judy likes to read fiction.
8. Joan will go to a prestigious college.
9. The court should rule for the defendant.
10. The president spoke at our school.

Answers

1. John, Cindy's boyfriend, went to the new production of *Romeo and Juliet* with Larry and me.
2. Mark, our baby, played with his red truck.
3. The summer sun set slowly in the west, creating a myriad of reds and yellows.
4. The schoolchildren enjoyed the band concert, which featured Sousa marches.
5. After dinner, we watched *Criminal Minds* and *CSI*.
6. I crammed for the torts exam for six hours.
7. Judy, an English major, likes to read 19th-century novels.
8. Joan, my best friend, will attend Yale next fall.
9. This court should grant the defendant's motion for summary judgment.
10. President Obama spoke about leadership at our college graduation.

Exercise 9-4

Identify the sentence patterns for the following sentences.

1. Even though he was tired, Vlad went to the party.
2. The brief was written by Maria.
3. Perez threw the ball to Dieter.
4. The orchestra played works by Wagner, Beethoven, and Schubert.
5. Leslie did well on the exam, although she didn't study much.
6. The court lacked subject matter jurisdiction over the case because the plaintiff and the defendant were from the same state.
7. After the rain, the sun broke through the clouds.
8. We went to see *Jersey Boys*, then we went to dinner.
9. We attended the party and the ball.
10. The children went to the park; afterwards, they ate lunch at Jimmy's house.

Answers

1. Complex sentence, consisting of a dependent clause and an independent clause.

2. Simple sentence, passive voice.
3. Simple sentence with a direct object and a prepositional phrase.
4. Simple sentence.
5. Complex sentence, consisting of an independent clause and a dependent clause.
6. Complex sentence, consisting of an independent clause and a dependent clause.
7. Simple sentence. "After the rain" is a prepositional clause.
8. Compound sentence linked by a comma and a conjunction.
9. Simple sentence.
10. Compound sentence linked by a linking adverb.

Exercise 9-5

Edit the following paragraph.

The plaintiff had several causes of action. The plaintiff alleged intentional misrepresentation and fraud in the purchase of a car. She also alleges revocation of acceptance and violation of the consumer protection act. The plaintiff alleged that the defendant had sold her a used car, representing that the engine had been recently rebuilt. She discovered that the engine had not been rebuilt. She discovered this fact when she had talked to her regular mechanic that she usually went to. The plaintiff requested rescission of the purchase. She also requested return of the purchase price that she had paid for the car. She also requested punitive damages and attorney's fees.

Answer

The plaintiff alleged fraud, revocation of acceptance, and violation of the consumer protection act in the purchase of a car. She claimed that the defendant had sold her a used car, representing that the engine had been recently rebuilt. However, when she talked to her regular mechanic, she discovered that the engine had not been rebuilt. The plaintiff requested rescission of the purchase, return of the purchase price, punitive damages, and attorney's fees.

Exercise 9-6

Edit the following paragraph.

Trademark protection exists on both the federal level and the state level. This is unlike patent law or copyright law, where federal law preempts state law. The main requirement for protection of trademarks is prior use. When a mark has been used, it can be registered with the Patent and Trademark Office. Infringement of trademarks depends on whether there is a likelihood of confusion between the allegedly infringing mark and the other mark. If there is a likelihood of confusion, then there is infringement. Remedies for redressing infringement include injunctive relief and monetary damages.

Answer

Trademark protection exists on both federal and state levels, unlike patent or copyright, where federal law preempts state law. The main requirement for trademark protection is prior use. Moreover, when a mark has been used, the owner can register it with the Patent and Trademark Office. Trademark infringement depends on whether there is a likelihood of confusion between the allegedly infringing mark and the other mark. Remedies for infringement include injunctive relief and damages.

Exercise 9-7

First identify the problems in the following sentences, then eliminate them.

1. Due to the fact that the federal budget did not balance, Congress raised taxes.
2. Mary was rather sure that her daughter would win the spelling bee.
3. Although the track was muddy, the race was won by Affrid, a speed horse.
4. The teacher's determination was that our exam would be oral.
5. Although the weather was cold, we swam in the lake.

6. Kate's prom dress was red in color.
7. The dress that the young bride wore was white.
8. The driver of the red car looked at the driver of the other car in an angry manner.
9. It is obvious that John is the best bowler on our team.
10. There are two theories of liability in this case: (1) negligence and (2) strict liability.
11. Margaret will go to the mall, and on the way home, she picked up dinner.
12. Bob had to have a milkshake.
13. The president made full disclosure of his tax returns a week before the election.
14. Smith was selected as a member the Olympic team.
15. The doctor was concerned that the condition would recur again.
16. Marcia committed a violation of the Act by her failure to file a Q-455 form.
17. Jim likes 19th-century sculpture and 20th-century sculpture.
18. The decoration of the gym was done by Julie and Mark.
19. He glanced at the beautiful model in a shy manner.
20. I was helped in my move by Pat and Sandy.

Answers

1. Because the federal budget did not balance, Congress raised taxes. (wordiness)
2. Mary was sure that her daughter would win the spelling bee. (unnecessary qualifier)
3. Although the track was muddy, Affrid, a speed horse, won the race. (passive voice)
4. The teacher decided that our exam would be oral. (nominalization)
5. Correct.
6. Kate's prom dress was red. (wordiness)
7. The young bride wore a white dress. (wordiness; long descriptive phrase)

8. The red car's driver glared at the driver of the other car. (write with verbs, wordiness) (I did not change "driver of the other car" to create variety.)
9. John is the best bowler on our team. (wordiness)
10. Correct.
11. Margaret will go to the mall, and, on the way home, she will pick up dinner. (inconsistent verb tenses)
12. Bob needed a milkshake. (complex verb construction)
13. The president fully disclosed his tax returns a week before the election. (nominalization)
14. The committee selected Smith as a member of the Olympic team. (passive voice)
15. The doctor was concerned that the condition would recur. (wordiness)
16. Marcia violated the Act by failing to file a Q-455 form. (nominalizations)
17. Jim like 19th- and 20th-century sculpture. (wordiness)
18. Julie and Mark decorated the gym. (passive voice, nominalization)
19. He shyly glanced at the beautiful model. (wordiness)
20. Pat and Sandy helped me move. (passive voice)

Note: There are multiple solutions on some of the above exercises. A good writer considers all solutions, then picks the one that best conveys his meaning.

Exercise 9-8

Answer the following questions about the small-scale paradigm.

1. Write out the small-scale paradigm.
2. Why does the paradigm start with the conclusion?
3. Why does the law begin with the rule?
4. What is the purpose of the rule explanation?
5. What belongs in the rule explanation?
6. What is a rule illustration?

7. How would you organize a rule illustration?
8. What is the most important thing about the rule illustration?
9. What is the application section?
10. What are the parts of the application section?
11. What is the purpose of the rule application?
12. What is the most important thing to remember about the rule application?
13. What is the case comparison?
14. How do you organize a case comparison?
15. Name the places you can put counterargument.
16. How is the small-scale paradigm a synthesis of the law?

Answers

For the answers to most of these exercises, refer to Chapter 7.

8. To find cases that are close to the facts of your case.
12. Apply the law to the facts *in detail*.
16. The rule is a synthesis of the holdings of all the relevant cases. You should synthesize the rule explanation from several cases.

Exercise 9-9

Answer the following questions about large- and medium-scale organization.

1. How do you organize on the large-scale level if there are multiple issues?
2. What is the key to organization on the large- and medium-scale levels if there are not multiple issues?
3. How can you articulate large-and medium-scale organization?
4. What are the most important aspects of an introduction?
5. What should headings and subheadings in an objective memorandum usually include?
6. Why are the headings in a brief often called point headings?
7. What should headings and subheadings in a brief usually contain?

8. What is the purpose of thesis paragraphs?
9. What is the best organization for a thesis paragraph?
10. Why is closure important?
11. What is the function of a conclusion?
12. How would you structure a conclusion?
13. Can you include new material in a conclusion?
14. Create a chart showing how all the parts fit together.

Answers

1. Put the issues in a logical order. Logical orders include (1) put threshold issues first, (2) put the issues in order of cause of action, and (3) put most important issues first.
2. Organize by the law. Take the rule and break it into its parts. When you can't logically break it down into another level, use the small-scale paradigm. Leave out any part or subpart of the rule that is not in dispute.
3. With introductions, headings and subheadings, thesis paragraphs, closure, and conclusions.
4. An introduction should introduce the issues in dispute and set up the discussion or argument section's organization.
5. Both the law and the facts. Also, they should be as focused on what is in dispute.
6. Because they are arguments.
7. They should generally contain the conclusion, the law, the facts, and the reasoning.
8. To set up sections and subsections that have multiple parts.
9. Like a mini analysis: conclusion, law, application (analysis).
10. Because it creates space between sections, subsections, and sub-subsections.
11. To sum up the argument or discussion section.
12. Based on the organization of the body.
13. You usually don't include new material in a conclusion.
14. See Chapter 8.

Exercise 9-10

Edit the following paragraphs and identify the major problem(s) with the paragraphs.

1. Should a child be compensated in damages for loss of parental consortium? Prior to 1980, not a single state had allowed any recovery for a loss of parental consortium by a child. Since 1980, at least seven jurisdictions have given monetary damages for a child's loss of parental consortium. However, during the same period, an equal number of states have refused to recognize loss of parental consortium as a valid cause of action. This paper will discuss the emergence of compensation for loss of parental consortium and evaluate the true wisdom of permitting monetary recovery for loss of parental consortium. Previous articles on loss of parental consortium have either advocated complete and entire recovery or none at all. The actual, correct position may be a compromise between these two extremes: allowing compensation for certain specific elements of loss of consortium and denying it for other specific elements of loss of consortium.

Answer

Should a child be compensated for loss of parental consortium? Prior to 1980, no state had allowed recovery for loss of parental consortium. Since 1980, at least seven jurisdictions have given such damages. However, during the same period, an equal number of states have refused to recognize this cause of action. This paper will discuss the emergence of compensation for loss of parental consortium and evaluate the wisdom of permitting such recovery. Previous articles on loss of parental consortium have either advocated complete recovery or none at all. The correct position may be a compromise between these extremes: allowing compensation for certain elements of loss of consortium and denying it for others. (wordiness and lack of variety or overuse of a phrase)

2. A cause of action for loss of parental consortium has emerged only since 1980. It is important to look at the history of compensation for loss of other types of consortium to show the policies underlying compensation for loss of parental consortium. A husband was allowed to recover for tortuous injury to his wife at common law. The recovery of the husband included damages for loss of sexual relations, society, and affection. He recovered medical expenses he incurred on his wife's behalf. A wife did not have a cause of action for loss of consortium at common law. The husband had complete control over his wife's property. He was entitled to her custody, services, and conjugal affection. A wife could not sue unless her husband was also a party. The wife did not have the capacity to sue unless her husband joined as a plaintiff.

Answer

Because a cause of action for loss of parental consortium has emerged only since 1980, it is important to look at the history of compensation for loss of other types of consortium to show the policies underlying such compensation. At common law, a husband was allowed to recover for tortuous injury to his wife. His recovery included damages for loss of sexual relations, society, and affection, as well as medical expenses he incurred on his wife's behalf. A wife did not have a similar action at common law. The reasons for this were twofold. First, the husband had complete control over his wife's property and was entitled to her custody, services, and conjugal affection. Second, the wife lacked the capacity to sue unless her husband joined as a plaintiff. (coherence, choppiness, repetitive sentence, and wordiness)

3. Following the common law of England, the right of the wife to recover for loss of her husband's consortium was not recognized by early American decisions. In 1950, an action for loss of a husband's consortium was created by the District of Columbia Circuit Court in order to achieve equality between the sexes. Since 1950, most of the courts have followed this holding, although a few jurisdictions have obtained equality by denying damages to both spouses of the marriage.

On the other hand, compensation for loss of consortium has not been extended by most courts to unmarried couples.

Answer

Following English common law, early American decisions did not recognize a wife's right to recover for loss of her husband's consortium. In 1950, the District of Columbia Circuit created an action for loss of a husband's consortium in order to achieve equality between the sexes. Since 1950, most courts have followed this holding, although a few jurisdictions have obtained equality by denying damages to both spouses. On the other hand, most courts have not extended compensation for loss of consortium to unmarried couples. (passive voice and wordiness)

4. Several commentators advocated compensation for loss of parental consortium in the 1970s, but *Ferriter v. Daniel O'Connell's Sons, Inc.* was the first case to compensate for these kinds of losses. In *Ferriter*, the father of two minor children was paralyzed when he was struck in the neck by a heavy wooden beam. He was injured while working for the defendant as a carpenter. His spouse and children filed suit to recover for loss of spousal consortium and parental consortium. They also filed suit for mental anguish. The trial court granted the motion of the defendant for summary judgment on the mental anguish claims. It denied the motion for both consortium claims. The Supreme Judicial Court of Massachusetts upheld the lower court's rulings on the consortium claims. It reversed on the mental anguish claims.

Answer

Although several commentators advocated compensation for loss of parental consortium in the 1970s, *Ferriter v. Daniel O'Connell's Sons, Inc.* was the first case to compensate for these losses. In *Ferriter*, the father of two minor children was paralyzed when he was struck in the neck by a heavy wooden beam while working for the defendant as a carpenter. His spouse and children filed suit to recover for loss of spousal and parental consortium, as well as mental anguish. The trial court granted the defendant's motion for summary judgment on the mental anguish claims, and denied the motion for both consortium claims. The Supreme Judicial Court of Massachusetts upheld the lower court's rulings on the consortium claims, but reversed on the mental anguish claims. (emphasis, choppiness, and wordiness)

5. The appellate court made the acknowledgment that a minor child has a deep and strong interest in his own parent's society, an interest closely analogous to the interest of a wife. The wrongful death statute recognizes the right of the child to recover for loss of parental society, and it is entirely appropriate to protect the child's reasonable expectation of parental society when the parent suffers negligent injury rather than death. The court's conclusion was that the Ferriter children could claim for loss of consortium, if they could make the demonstration that they were minors dependent on their father not only for economic needs, but also for filial needs of closeness, guidance, and nurture.

Answer

The appellate court acknowledged that a minor child has a strong interest in his parent's society, an interest closely analogous to that of a wife. The wrongful death statute recognizes a child's right to recover for loss of parental society, and it is appropriate to protect the child's reasonable expectation of parental society when the parent suffers negligent injury rather than death. The court concluded that the Ferriter children could recover for loss of consortium, if they could demonstrate that they were minors dependent on their father not only for economic needs, but also for filial needs of closeness, guidance, and nurture. (nominalizations and wordiness)

6. The above cases giving compensation for loss of consortium constitute persuasive authority and strong arguments. Several jurisdictions have rejected actions for loss of parental consortium since 1980. The case of *Zorgos v. Rosen* denied recovery. The court thought it was wise to leave the decision to the legislature. It was further stated by the

court that, since the legislature has recognized the right of the child to recover in an action for wrongful death but not when the parent is only injured, the legislature has made the deliberate choice not to create this cause of action. Note that this reasoning is exactly and directly opposite that of *Hibpsham* case mentioned above.

Answer

Despite the above cases, several jurisdictions have rejected actions for loss of parental consortium since 1980. *Zorgos v. Rosen* denied recovery because the court thought it was wise to leave the decision to the legislature. The court further stated that, since the legislature has recognized a child's right to recover in a wrongful death action but not when the parent is only injured, the legislature has deliberately chosen not to create this cause of action. (Note that this reasoning is exactly opposite that of *Hibpsham* mentioned above.) (treading water, emphasis, choppiness, continuity, passive voice, and nominalization)

7.   Cases like *Hibpsham* and *Theama* have countered standard arguments against recovery for loss of consortium, but Judge Levin in his dissent in *Berger* raised objections that extend to the very basis of compensation for loss of parental consortium. Initially, Judge Levin first looked to the history of actions for loss of consortium. He finds that they had their origin in a husband's proprietary rights in the services of his wife. Equality between husband and wife caused the action for loss of consortium to be extended to the wife, although it could just as easily have been achieved simply by abolishing the rights of the husband, as a few states did. Since the soundness of the first step—giving a wife the same consortium rights as her husband—has been questioned, there is no reason at all to proceed further along the same path (extending recovery to a child's claim) merely because it seems to be logical.

Answer

While cases like *Hibpsham* and *Theama* have countered standard arguments against recovery for loss of consortium, Judge Levin in his dissent in *Berger* raised objections that extend to the basis of compensation for loss of parental consortium. Judge Levin first looked to the history of actions for loss of consortium, finding that they had their origin in a husband's proprietary rights in his wife's services. Equality between husband and wife caused the action for loss of consortium to be extended to the wife, although it could just as easily have been achieved by abolishing the husband's rights (as a few states did). Since the soundness of the first step (giving a wife the same consortium rights as her husband) has been questioned, there is no reason to proceed further along the same path (extending recovery to a child's claim) merely because it seems logical. (emphasis, wordiness, and abrupt change of verb tense)

8.   The dissent of Justice Levin suggests that a newly constructed approach to the determination of whether or not loss of parental consortium should be compensable might be necessary. Cases and commentators have adopted an all-or-nothing approach. A middle approach that gives compensation for tangible economic injury while denying recovery for intangible emotional support negates many of the specific criticisms that are involved with the all-or-nothing approach.

Answer

Justice Levin's dissent suggests that a new approach to determining whether loss of parental consortium should be compensable might be necessary. To date, cases and commentators have adopted an all-or-nothing approach. A middle approach that compensates for tangible economic injury while denying recovery for intangible emotional support negates many of the criticisms involved with the all-or-nothing approach. (wordiness, continuity, and nominalization)

9.   Tort law is moving away from compensating for interferences with relational interests. Only a small number of jurisdictions give recognition to such intentional torts as alienation of affections or retain criminal conversation as a crime. Courts have been more reluctant to protect the relationship of parent and child than the relationship of

husband and wife. It seems to be illogical to develop a new tort for negligent interference with a relational interest (loss of parental love and affection), while rejecting old torts. It is absurd to give a child damages for the loss of a parent's love and companionship that is negligently caused, while denying similar recovery when such loss is intentionally caused by alienation of affections.

Answer

Courts should deny damages for the intangible support part of loss of parental consortium. First, tort law is moving away from compensating for interferences with relational interests. Only a few jurisdictions recognize such intentional torts as alienation of affections or retain criminal conversation as a crime. Second, courts have been more reluctant to protect the relationship of parent and child than that of husband and wife. Finally, it seems illogical to develop a new tort for negligent interference with a relational interest (loss of parental love and affection), while rejecting old ones. It is absurd to give a child damages for the loss of a parent's love and companionship that is negligently caused, while denying similar recovery when such loss is intentionally caused by alienation of affections. (needs topic sentence, organization/coherence, wordiness, nominalization, and overuse of certain words)

10. There are many reasons to deny compensation for loss of parental consortium. Reasons for denying compensation for loss of parental consortium include deference to the legislature, the possibility of multiple litigation, the danger of double recovery, consortium's historical origins, and its being an injury to a relational interest. None of these reasons applies to the economic aspects of parental consortium. Courts compensate for similar economic injuries every day without waiting for the legislature to act. Often courts use deference to the legislature as an excuse when they don't want to act. Multiple litigation can be avoided by requiring the child to join her claim to that of the parent, as the *Hibpsham* court suggested. The jury can be carefully instructed to avoid double recovery. Instructions on damages are an integral part

of instructions in a jury case anyway. Recovery for economic injury does not involve the need for justification of the historical origins of consortium. The economic loss to the child is a direct injury rather than an injury to a relationship.

Answer

Reasons for denying compensation for loss of parental consortium include (1) deference to the legislature, (2) the possibility of multiple litigation, (3) the danger of double recovery, (4) consortium's historical origins, and (5) its being an injury to a relational interest. None of these reasons applies to the economic aspects of parental consortium. First, courts compensate for similar economic injuries every day without waiting for the legislature to act. (Often courts use deference to the legislature as an excuse when they don't want to act.) Second, courts can avoid multiple litigation by requiring the child to join her claim to that of the parent, as *Hibpsham* suggested. Third, the court can carefully instruct the jury to avoid double recovery. (Instructions on damages are an integral part of instructions in a jury case anyway.) Fourth, recovery for economic injury does not require justification of consortium's historical origins. Finally, the child's economic loss is a direct injury rather than an injury to a relationship. (treading water, organization, wordiness, continuity, emphasis, and overuse of passive voice)

Wrap Up

Has my writing improved by using this book? In what ways has my writing improved? What things do I need to work on more?

Can I see both the large and small picture? Can I see how a holistic approach to writing and knowledge of the mechanics of writing work together? Am I now a reader-oriented writer? Do I try to stand in my reader's shoes? Have I become a detailed-oriented writer? Do I think about every word I have written?

Has the book had a practical effect on my writing? Has my brief writing improved? Do I write clearer arguments?

Improving your writing is a lifelong task. One way to keep improving your learning is to reflect on your writing each time you finish a major task. Did I write the best brief I am capable of? Will my reader have any problems understanding what I have written? Did I employ an efficient approach?

Good luck in your future writing!

Glossary

Active voice
: when the subject of the sentence is the doer of the action; actor (noun or pronoun)–verb–supporting material.

Adjective
: part of speech; a word that modifies a noun or pronoun.

Adverb
: part of speech; a word that modifies a verb, adjective, or adverb.

Article
: a type of adjective that makes a noun specific (the) or indefinite (a, an).

Clause
: a group of words containing a subject and a verb that is part of a sentence.

Coherence
: when the sentences (or paragraphs) fit together.

Colon
: a punctuation mark used after a statement that introduces an explanation, an example, a quotation, or a series (:).

Complex sentence
: a sentence that comprises a dependent clause and an independent clause.

Compound sentence
> a sentence that consists of two (or more) independent clauses.

Conjunction
> part of speech; words that join words, phrases, and clauses, e.g., and, or, etc.

Conjunctive adverbs
> adverbs that act as a transition between complete ideas; also called linking adverbs, e.g., however, furthermore, nevertheless, etc.

Continuity
> thematic connections between sentences (or paragraphs).

Dash
> a punctuation mark that sets off a word or phrase after an independent clause or sets off a parenthetical remark (e.g., words, phrases, or clauses that interrupt a sentence).

Demonstrative adjectives
> an adjective that points out the item it is referring to.

Dependent clause
> a part of a sentence; a dependent clause cannot stand on its own.

Direct object
> a noun or pronoun that receives the action of the verb or shows the result of the action.

Distinguishing cases
> a type of reverse analogy; showing that the facts of the precedent case are not like the facts of the present case to convince a court that the rule from the precedent case does not apply to the present case. The facts of A are not like the facts of B, so the rule from A does not apply to B. Can also be done with policy distinctions.

Empty sentences
> sentences that don't add anything; they are just unnecessary filler.

Flow
> the connections between sentences (or paragraphs). Flow is broader than continuity in that flow can be created by techniques like transitional words, combining sentences, listening, etc.

Independent clause
> a part of a sentence; an independent clause can stand alone as a sentence.

Indirect object
> precedes the direct object and tells to whom or for whom the action of the verb is done and who is receiving the direct object.

Large-scale organization
> organization of the discussion of an objective memo, the argument of a brief, a chapter, an essay, etc.

Medium-scale organization
> organization of sections and subsections.

Misplaced modifier
> a word or phrase describing something but not placed close enough to the word it modifies.

Nominalization
> using a noun or an adjective in place of a verb.

Noun
> part of speech; a word that signifies a person, place, thing, action, idea, condition, or quality.

Paragraph unity
> when all the sentences in a paragraph are on the same subject, and all the sentences relate to the topic sentence.

Participial phrase
> a phrase in which a verb is employed as an adjective by adding "-ing."

Passive voice
> a sentence (or clause) in which the subject is being acted upon.

Personal pronoun
> a pronoun that takes the place of a specific person or thing.

Phrase
> a group of words, acting as a part of speech, that does not express a complete thought. A phrase does not contain both a noun and a verb.

Policy-based reasoning
> making a legal judgment based on what rule would work best from a practical point of view or for society as a whole.

Preposition
> part of speech; a word that relates a noun or pronoun to another word in the sentence.

Prepositional phrase
> a phrase that begins with a preposition and ends with a noun or pronoun that relates the noun or pronoun to the rest of the sentence.

Pronoun
> a word that takes the place of a noun.

Reasoning by analogy
> reasoning by similarities. The facts of the precedent case are like the facts of the present case, so the rule from the precedent case should apply to the present case. You can also reason by analogy based on policy.

Semicolon
> a punctuation mark that connects independent clauses and creates a closer relationship than a period does (;).

Simple sentence
> a sentence consisting of a noun and a verb with or without additional modifying words and a direct and/or indirect object. This is the most common sentence pattern.

Small-scale paradigm
> a way of organizing a simple analysis of an issue or a subissue (see Chapter 7).

Subsidiary ideas
> less important ideas.

Supporting or subsidiary clause
> a clause that contains subsidiary ideas.

Thesis paragraph
> a paragraph that introduces a section or subsection.

Topic sentence
> a sentence that presents the main idea of the paragraph; usually the first sentence.

Transitional phrase

a phrase that connects (shows the relationship between) two sentences or two paragraphs, e.g., to the contrary, while in prison, during her testimony, in the next case.

Transitional word

a word that connects two sentences or two paragraphs, e.g., next, after, therefore, yet, however, likewise, also, moreover, etc.

Transitional sentence

a sentence that connects two paragraphs.

Treading water

using filler to make your writing longer.

Verb

part of speech; a word that expresses an action or a condition of a subject.